THE INHUMAN
CONDITION

Keith Tester

London and New York

First published 1995
by Routledge
11 New Fetter Lane, London EC4P 4EE

Simultaneously published in the USA and Canada
by Routledge
29 West 35th Street, New York, NY 10001

© 1995 Keith Tester

Typeset in Palatino by LaserScript, Mitcham, Surrey
Printed and bound in Great Britain by
T.J. Press (Padstow) Ltd, Padstow, Cornwall

British Library Cataloguing in Publication Data
A catalogue record for this book is available from the British Library

Library of Congress Cataloguing in Publication Data
A catalogue record for this book has been requested

ISBN 0–415–10731–8 (hbk)
ISBN 0–415–10732–6 (pbk)

CONTENTS

THE INHUMAN CONDITION

In *The Inhuman Condition* Keith Tester explores whether we are capable of coming to terms with the world we have made. He argues that we are not. We are so confused by the wonders and the sights and sounds around us that we all try to build safe little homes in which we can, for a while, be consoled by love which is doomed to fail as soon as it is thought about and by commodities which leave us unsatisfied. We all try to make sense of our humanity by turning elsewhere: to inhuman things. All of us, that is, with enough money.

The book offers a major interpretation of contemporary cultural and social relationships. It is also a major exercise in sociology which encompasses thinkers like Heidegger, Arendt, Benjamin and Simmel. The author opens with Heidegger worrying about photographs of the earth and argues that, contrary to sociological orthodoxy, the world is now more experienced in the finding than the making. Tester then explores aspects of that finding: from the beautiful promises of commodities to the noises and sights of cities, from the search for love to the throbbing gristle painted by Francis Bacon. We can only come to terms with our experiences and our existence if we embrace the inhuman idiot wisdom of kitsch; and perhaps there is no escape from the embrace of stupidity.

Keith Tester is Reader in Social and Cultural Theory at the University of Portsmouth.

INTRODUCTION

Why is it that the social and cultural worlds, which would not exist were it not for the actions of men and women, are experienced as almost concrete monoliths which stand over and above individuals, shaping everything they (we) do and think? How can it be that the things which we make tend to be experienced rather more like things which we find? By what means have social and cultural arrangements and relationships come to seem to be quite natural and, in fact, not social and cultural at all? Why do so many people feel so perplexed and dissatisfied and why do so many people invest all their hopes in the search for love?

These are the kinds of questions which this book seeks to pose and answer. They are some of the most important general issues which must be considered if it is hoped to develop any significant interpretation of the worlds we inhabit and experience. These questions are also important because with their answers they go a considerable way towards helping to provide an understanding of what moral duties, obligations and responsibilities the individual might have in relationships with others. Consequently, although this book is largely constructed along the fault line between sociological and more philosophical lines of enquiry, its main concern and motivation is predominantly ethical. At a fairly crass empirical level, I am worried that most of us actually do not seem to care too much about what happens to (some) other people because we are too concerned about what we are doing in our everyday existences (such that we might not buy coffee produced by a workers' co-operative simply because coffee produced for a multinational which dumps baby milk in the 'Third World' is so much cheaper). I want to try to understand why most of us are so often unable or unprepared to broaden our moral and human horizons beyond our everyday routines. I want to try to work out if it makes any sense to carry on talking about something as valuable but, seemingly, as improbable as the human condition. Additionally, I want to try to work out what the human condition might be in a world which tends to be experienced as something which is found and not at all made.

I have already used the word 'experience' with some frequency. Throughout this book I use the word in an immensely untheorized way. For my purposes, experience refers to: firstly, the act of living through an event, events or processes and reflecting on it or them and, secondly, the existential effect on the individual of those events or processes (how the individual is situated and positioned as a subject of social and cultural relationships). As such, one of the main concerns of this book is to try to provide an interpretation of the processes, relationships and arrangements which give the individual a sense of 'embeddedness' in the world.

In this book I pursue the possibility that individuals embed themselves and are embedded in the world to the extent that the world is experienced as something which is like nature and most certainly enchanted. With this line of enquiry I am rather tending to set myself against the dominant narratives of modern sociology. I am increasingly convinced that while it is possible and important to write and talk about social and cultural relationships, writing and talking can have little or nothing to do with orthodox academic sociology if it is to remain interesting and insightful. The discipline of sociology has been constructed around what might be called the 'productivist paradigm'. This paradigm presupposes that the social world (which is reified and ordered by the imaginative and thereafter allegedly scientific concept of 'society') is a social and cultural production. In Marx that production is one of material relationships and goods, in Weber the production is one of rationalization, in Durkheim the production is one of moral order. The authorized readings within the discipline of sociology all tend to emphasize these aspects of the work of the 'founding figures' and desperately try to deny other readings or other founders.

But I want to suggest that perhaps this productivist paradigm only tells one from amongst a range of possible stories and, for that matter, only the story which is compatible with the myth of modernity as, in the words of Kant, 'man's emergence from his self-incurred immaturity'. In this book I want to pursue the distinct likelihood that it is possible to write another kind of story about social and cultural relationships, a story about a process in which the world is experienced not in the making but, quite the contrary, in the finding. I want to write a sociology which pursues the possibility that we do not live in a disenchanted world but rather that we live in a world which tends to be experienced precisely as enchanted. The enchantment might surround the promises of happiness made in the name of a commodity, the tricks of sexual expertise contained in a book or video, the sense of loss of self in the oceanic eyes of another which is called love. As such, what I am proposing is that in so far as it is the slave of the productivist paradigm, the discipline of sociology tells a story of disenchantment which might well have decreasing (or little, if it ever had any) resonance with the experiences of men and women.

The corollary of this is that I am also muddying the sacred sociological distinction between the social or the cultural and the natural. I want to propose that in so far as the world is experienced as enchanted, so it is also likely to be experienced as quite natural and not as social and cultural at all. And our lives do seem to be natural to a greater or a lesser extent; if they did not they would be apprehended as utterly contingent, utterly artificial and, therefore, of little or no authority, legitimacy and foundation. If we do not construct our lives as somewhat natural and as partially (or largely) inevitable, it is scarcely likely that our lives will hold any purpose or reason for us (other than a Camus-type reason of the absence of reason; a situation in which life has a purpose precisely because it has no purpose). That sense of nature is associated with processes and relationships of enchantment; enchantment gives meaning because it implies an ultimate and ineffable order beyond our wildest dreams.

Obviously, the book operates at a fairly high level of generality and abstraction. This is a deliberate choice on my part. I have opted for abstraction so that it might be possible to develop a narrative which, not to put too fine a point on the matter, can be used as a stick with which to beat actual relationships and practices. I have opted for a general speculative approach so that it is possible to do something rather more useful than just describe everyday life and its experiences (and if those descriptions emphasize the importance of activities like shopping to the exclusion of all else they are little more than magic books for the world of enchantment; they are symptoms). The narrative mode of this book represents my attempt to move beyond simple commentary on the empirical and, instead, to try to interpret its conditions of existence and moral implications. I have tried to develop an analysis which opens up the world.

I am using generality to constitute a narrative which might be able to develop a critique. The purpose of that critique is not at all to tell others the absolute universal truth. It is not at all to lead everyone into the light which I alone of all mortals presently enjoy. My critical intention is a lot more modest that that. I am not trying to develop a critique so that I might find the brightly lit path to some Never-never Land called 'more object-adequate theory'. I am trying to develop a critique in order to demonstrate that things are not the way they must be. My 'method' of critique has two main aims. Firstly, it is intended to inject just a little irony into social and cultural relationships; I want to highlight the possibility that things might well be other than they appear. Secondly, it is intended to imply a case for human social and cultural possibility rather than just necessity. This book tries to provide one story of how human possibilities have been transformed into necessities, precisely so that possibility might become possible.

This book offers a sociology which seeks to provide an interpretation of how the world has come to be experienced as simply the way the world has to be. But by showing that the world became this way it can be implied that the world might be able to be made to become something different; or at least that the world might be experienced in different ways. This book tries to offer a sociology which does not preclude possibility. In this way, it modestly offers a sociology which has the immodest intention of standing in the way of the dehumanization of the social and cultural milieu. As Kurt Wolff said (in an immensely Schutzian vein which I do not necessarily share; I share Wolff's conclusion but not necessarily his way of getting to it):

> If we, sociologists or not, but we sociologists too, trust our senses, rather than the received notions that blind them, and thus us, to reality, the only way we can begin coming to terms with our "paramount reality" is to say No to it, for, as Herbert Marcuse put it, "The whole is the truth, and the whole is false".
>
> (Wolff 1989: 326)

I hope that this book will play a small part in showing that, about social and cultural relationships, the last word should never, ever, be said. And so this book does not claim to tell anything as inhuman as the 'truth'.

I have just used the word 'inhuman'. I have also spoken about dehumanization. These words need some definition. A sense of the problem of the inhuman and of the process of dehumanization runs through this entire book. It is precisely this sense which lends the book its moral commitment and, indeed, a considerable part of its formal properties. Perhaps the best way of grasping what I mean when I talk about the inhuman and dehumanization is to provide a little detail about what I take it to mean to be human. And one of the best ways of doing that is to quote Ortega y Gasset. He nicely makes the point I would make less nicely. In a somewhat existentialist proposition Ortega says that the individual has a duty to himself to make himself. As Ortega puts it: 'I invent projects of being and doing in the light of circumstance. This alone I come upon, this alone is given me: circumstance.' He continues:

> Whether he be original or a plagiarist, man is the novelist of himself. . . . Among . . . possibilities I must choose. Hence, I am free. But, be it well understood, I am free by compulsion, whether I wish to be or not. . . . To be free means to be lacking in constitutive identity, not to have subscribed to a determined being, to be able to be other than what one was.
> (Ortega quoted in Kermode 1973: 220)

Inhuman is everything which forces the individual to 'subscribe to a determined being'. Inhuman is everything which gives the individual the already written script of the novel she or he is going to be able to write. Dehumanization is the processual tendency of circumstance to foreclose on the possibilities which the individual experiences him or her self as having in relation to the situations she or he is thrown into. Yet the profound difficulty is that precisely without these circumstances and experiential determinations, the world could scarcely be a place of and for human being. The human and the inhuman can never be separated. They are like Siamese twins who cannot be cut away from each other. The making of the human world creates domains of the inhuman and it implies processes of dehumanization.

If anyone has read my book *The Life and Times of Post-Modernity* they will quickly recognize that this book is a continuation of themes and problems which were explored there. If *The Life and Times* ended up suggesting that ethical relationships might have collapsed and that sociology has quite possibly been complicit in that collapse, this book is motivated by an attempt to see whether there is any possibility that responsibility can be reconstituted on a human terrain and, more implicitly, whether sociology might have any role to play in that reconstitution. But anyone who compares the two books will notice that my terminology is now a little different. Most obviously, this book does not explicitly talk about post-modernity. But this book implicitly talks about post-modernity on virtually every page. *The Life and Times* interprets post-modernity as a specific and particular social and cultural position which is not at all universal. Where then does this leave supposedly universal ethics? What then is the orbit of my moral responsibilities? What is the terrain of my political action?

These kinds of questions were brought home to me through an experience of everyday life; and a very ordinary experience at that. They were brought home to me during a walk along the Palace Pier in Brighton. I would recommend anyone who believes that post-modernity is a universal condition to take a walk along the Pier and ask themselves 'What does post-modernity mean here?' The only answer I could come up with was: 'absolutely nothing' (and this answer itself leads to further questions about the relationship between categories in sociological narratives and social and cultural life). Perhaps it might be said that this book is written about post-modernity whilst standing beside the roundabout at the end of the Palace Pier (and so this book reeks with the smell and the flavour of fish and chips covered with tomato ketchup).

The Palace Pier is a place which runs through my experience of who and what I am. Every time I visit the Pier I find myself having to renegotiate my own identity and, indeed, my experience of self and the world. I guess that the Pier has such a great effect because when I was a boy it was a place of great pleasures, mysteries and wonder. It was so bright, loud, smelly. It was enchanted and enchanting. Now I am a little bit older, the Pier is a place almost of fear; it is still enchanted and enchanting but to very different effect than when I was a boy. The Pier is so bright, loud and smelly that I find it overwhelming, incomprehensible and almost terrifying. No doubt the panic of the Palace Pier is exacerbated because it punctures my sense and experiences of my social mobility. It returns me to the roots, roots I have struggled to keep at arms' length, in the Southern English working class; a class which has no traditions to bolster it, no landscape to nurture its memories (this working class is the product of migration and all the old houses and factories tend to be demolished as soon as they are obsolete); no sense of an escape route or, for that matter, any sense of a need for one. There was no alternative to the daily round of frustrated hopes and ambitions, material marginality (we were never poor enough to have a pride of suffering, never rich enough to buy a car). The only alternative was the pleasure symbolized by the Palace Pier. The Pier reminds me of everything I have tried desperately not to be; that is why its horror is so great, its pull so irresistible. In my experience of it, the Pier has moved from the wonder of enchantment to the fear of enchantment. (Clearly then, I can never be a latter day Richard Hoggart; I have no romance about the experiences and lives which the working class endure. I managed to get just enough to get out – just.) For me, the Pier represents an injury of class.

There is another reason why I have chosen not to foreground the word post-modernity. The word is like a red rag to a bull for some people. As soon as they see the word they dismiss an argument without a second thought and dismiss it as incoherent, insubstantial and of quite questionable propriety. The word post-modernity has become an obstacle to principled debate. Perhaps the debate can be conducted with a little more mutual respect if the word is jettisoned. But I have not at all thrown out the baby with that particular bath water.

The strategy I have adopted in order to try to interpret my experience and, at a more elevated level, to try to understand the possibilities of a post-modern human condition (here, then, post-modernity might be defined as the experiential and existential situation of the modern world become enchanted like nature and therefore as something to be overcome) is to develop a narrative which frequently refers to Hannah Arendt's book *The Human Condition* (1958). But my argument must not be read as an exegesis on Arendt (not least because I am not immodest enough to compare myself in any way with her). Instead, I use her book so often because it stands as one of the most masterly analyses of the implications of the situations of modernity on humanity and on individuals. Arendt offers a systematization of the modern world-view, the modern processes and the fate of the modern ambitions. I eschew the tendency towards systematic thinking (and towards system-building) and instead I use Arendt's book to speculate to what extent and in what ways a post-modern human condition might (or might not) diverge from the modern. If anything, my use of Arendt's wonderful book ought to be seen as a fairly pathetic exercise in an attempt to imitate Pierre Menard's rewrite of Don Quixote.

I have written a book which runs alongside Arendt's for another reason. I have wanted to highlight my belief that sociological narratives are not direct and somehow magisterial reflections of some reality, the truth of which exists 'out there' waiting to be discovered. Neither, therefore, can sociology be taken to stand as a report of the world. Sociology is a writing of the world and that writing takes place in terms of a mixture of experiences of self, experiences of being in the world, and experiences of other writings. As such, I want to emphasize that my encounter with Arendt is due to a combination of accident and inspiration. I did not have to read her book but when I did it endlessly provoked me; Arendt's book gave me pleasure. Neither then are the other texts I cite in this book regarded by me as absolute 'authorities'. Rather, I define them as inspirational partners in a dialogue. (These points summarize what I have been struggling to do for a couple of books now. I have been able to clarify my approach to sociology – in my own mind at least – thanks to Ann Game's revelation of the conceits of orthodox sociology writing; see Game 1991.) Fortunately for all of us, sociology can never come up with the last word (even though some sociologists might well presume that actually they can). Consequently, the dialectic of making and finding, and the experiences of finding not making, can be applied to sociology itself. This intellectual discipline does not, because it cannot, stand apart from the world it purports to understand.

Whatever merits this book might have are directly due to the people who kept me from complete stupidity when I was writing it. And so, as ever, thanks to Zygmunt Bauman, Chris Rojek and Linda Rutherford. For what it is worth, this book is dedicated to the memory of my dead father.

1

THINKING

When he first saw photographs of the earth, Martin Heidegger was frightened. He was frightened because, for him, the photographs suggested that now the world could function efficiently more or less independently of the designs and ambitions of humanity: 'everything is functioning and . . . the functioning drives us more and more to even further functioning, and . . . technology tears men loose from the earth and uproots them' (Heidegger 1993: 105). Heidegger continued to emphasize the impact of the photographs upon him: 'I do not know whether you were frightened, but I at any rate was frightened when I saw pictures coming from the moon to the earth' (Heidegger 1993: 105).

The pictures had effected a much greater destruction of the human relationship with the earth than any nuclear weapon could ever cause: 'We don't need any atom bomb. The uprooting of man has already taken place. The only thing we have left is purely technological relationships.' Simply: 'This is no longer the earth on which man lives' (Heidegger 1993: 105–106). The earth is no longer the earth because it is no longer the sole home of humanity; the pictures from the moon show that the earth has been transformed into just one home amongst a plurality of potential homes. For Heidegger, everything had been upset by the fact that the orbit of everything could be visualized without it having to be thought. Heidegger was expressing a sense of homesickness which, for him, urgently demanded some kind of reconstitution of home.

According to Heidegger the photographs mean that the time-honoured and legitimate relationships between humanity and the earth have been destroyed so that they can never be repaired: 'everything essential and everything great originated from the fact that man had a home and was rooted in a tradition' (Heidegger 1993: 106). But now humanity has become able to leave the earth on which it has been traditionally rooted (and rooted by tradition); now humanity can function on the moon (although, of course, and as Hans Jonas spotted, it is not humanity which functions in space but technology; humanity becomes the appendage to the machine; see Jonas 1984). The time-honoured since time immemorial home of humanity in the universe has been demolished and all that can be left in the ruins is the adoption of an attitude of readiness for the arrival of the god who can save us from what we ourselves have done, who can save us from what we ourselves have become. As Heidegger put it: 'The sole possibility that is left for us is to prepare a sort of readiness, through thinking and poetizing, for the appearance of the god or for the absence of the god in the time of foundering' (Heidegger 1993: 107).

Apart from the fears he made explicit, two other main themes can be seen to run through Heidegger's reaction to the pictures from the moon. Firstly, he was caused to see, recognize and acknowledge the immensely fragile if not trivial circumstances and foundation of the existence which had been the problem for a lifetime's intellectual endeavour. The meaning which had given his own life meaning was thrown into the pit of potential accident and cosmic insignificance. Secondly, Heidegger was caused to accept that the possibilities of human existence in and on the earth might well be of little compass in the universal order of things; the possibilities of human being and Being are closed down and made a lot less conceited when it is realized that, in relation to the universe, the earth is a rather small place.

Moreover, Heidegger was so frightened because the photographs of the earth implied a startling transformation of the relationship between humanity and the environment. Traditionally humanity is identified as a constituent part of some larger whole which is commonsensically constructed and perceived as having an objective reality all its own. Humanity is thus identified as one part amongst many in an equation. Humanity is not usually identified as the entire formula, even if the part allotted to humanity is understood to be defining and central to the whole. Additionally, the category of humanity is constructed as going on independently of the fates of any of the individuals who constitute it; I die but humanity lives after me; I am born and humanity takes me out of my simple physical compulsions.

2

But the photographs of the earth implied the possibility that all of these stable and taken for granted certainties could no longer be accepted without a second thought. On the one hand, a single man (or a small group of men all of whom could be named, all of whom lived in a single time and place – here and now) had taken a series of photographs which contained within it the whole extent of everything that humanity had done since time immemorial, and everything that humanity can ever do. A single man had been extracted from the continuity of humanity and, to some extent, made greater than it. He could gaze upon all the homes and all the achievements of all humanity in relation to the universe even though all humanity could never gaze upon him (if only for the simple reason that by the time the photographs were taken, humanity had been existing for a long time; a significant proportion of it had already died and another significant proportion was not yet born). On the other hand, technology, which was intended to provide a framework for the security and enrichment of human existence, had become able to contain all humanity within it; the artificial world of technology had become able to show that the human world is potentially relatively small and trivial.

This last point links up with Heidegger's important discussion of the enframing tendencies of technology. The photographs implied a containment of the meanings of the earth even as they also implied a freedom of humanity (or at least a freedom of individual men and women) from their natural home. But in that containment, the photographs also made the earth a problem to be dealt with; an opportunity to be exploited, a standing reserve waiting for animation by the designs and desires of humanity through technology. The photographs made the earth absolutely banal. Heidegger defines enframing as 'the gathering together which belongs to that setting-upon which challenges man and puts him in position to reveal the real, in the mode of ordering, as standing-reserve' (Heidegger 1978: 305). But humanity itself stands within the frame and not just outside of it. Indeed, for Heidegger, 'The frame holding sway means: the essence of man is framed, claimed, and challenged by a power which manifests itself in the essence of technology, a power which man himself does not control' (Heidegger 1993: 107).

But perhaps the problems of enframing go a little further. After all, if the earth is banal then so is humanity. But if humanity is able to enframe the earth then humanity itself cannot be as banal as the earth; but it is therefore and thereby quite homeless in the universe. The implication of all of this is immense: 'Philosophy is at an end' (Heidegger 1993: 107). What he meant by this rather trivial statement was that: 'the traditional metaphysical mode of thinking . . . no longer offers any possibility for experiencing in a thoughtful way the fundamental traits of the technological age, an age which is just beginning' (Heidegger 1993: 109). Hence the turn to thinking and poetry as strategies which 'would awaken, clarify, and fortify the readiness' required by the wait for a God who will almost certainly never arrive; or at least a God whose arrival cannot be guaranteed (Heidegger 1993: 110). Or, following Kafka, the God who will arrive the day after his coming.

Yet the ambivalent meanings of the photographs run much deeper than even all of this. It is tempting to suggest that the photographs of the earth are so problematic precisely because they throw us back onto our own resources to make any kind of sense of them. Thinking might make some sense of the photographs and of the general processes of technology. But even this activity does not hold out much hope for Heidegger. Firstly, thinking is difficult because it is a thoroughly ironic kind of activity: 'In the realm of thinking there are no authoritative assertions. The only measure for thinking is the matter which is itself to be thought. . . . Thinking has by reason of its own task put itself in a difficult situation' (Heidegger 1993: 114–115). Secondly, however, the activity of thinking is stuck in a situation where this reflexive attitude towards itself cannot arise; thinking is unable to think itself and, therefore, the world itself cannot be thought: 'no thinker speaks who is "great" enough to bring thinking immediately, and in a formative way, before its subject matter, and thereby to get it under way. For us contemporaries the greatness of what is to be thought is too great' (Heidegger 1993: 116). According to Heidegger then, humanity and the earth have been put into a situation of crisis and, if that was not bad enough, the thinking which might enable us to steel ourselves to our situation is in a state of crisis as well.

The photographs reduce the earth to the status of a thing to be looked at. But looking merely registers a presence which is accorded the status of existing prior to the moment of empirical observation and, therefore, prior to and independent of any

4

stories that it might be possible to construct in order to make some kind of sense of what it is that is seen. In themselves the photographs mean everything because actually they mean next to nothing. (To this extent it might be proposed that the photographs of the earth have much the same epistemological and ontological status as Abraham Zapruder's home movie of the Kennedy assassination. The images show absolutely everything and narrate absolutely nothing. They are, in their own way, quite pornographic.) Perhaps it is this fundamental meaninglessness of the orbit of all meaning which runs through Heidegger's concern and motivates his fear.

It is certainly the case that a number of conflicting senses can be made of the pictures from the moon. These radically different senses are not the idle products of idle intellectual games. Rather, their very multiplicity can be taken to be an indication of the major problem which human being in the world has become. Heidegger's analysis of technology as enframing leads to a reading of the photographs which implies that humanity has become the master of the universe; the master who can change the universal conditions of existence and not just the now little, now local circumstances in which men and women find themselves (circumstances which have been rendered little and local where once they were large and universal because now humanity can go to the moon. The possibility of movement outside the planet has transformed apprehensions of space and significance to such an extent that perhaps we are consigned to irony. Now it is indeed true to say that our problems do not amount to a hill of beans. But they are still our problems and they cannot be put in the lap of anyone else; there is no one else).

Yet the gain in enframing ability (in an ability to make the world) is predicated on the implication of the photographs that in the first instance at least the earth is simply there, waiting to be found. The world becomes independent of us and seemingly indifferent towards us even though all of our attention is focused upon it. The photographs which make us greater than the world we inhabit also establish the world as something we can only see as if through a window. The enframing of the earth by the technological mechanism of the pictures makes the status of humanity a question which cannot be answered very readily: controllers or by-standers? Makers or finders? Everything or nothing? Enframer of enframed? The photographs raise all of these questions about the meaning of humanity and they offer no answers whatsoever. They throw us back onto our own resources; resources which the photographs deprive of any conventional authority.

Martin Heidegger is not alone in registering disquiet at the ability of technology to picture the earth and thus turn the planet into something which can be enframed rather than letting it remain as the precondition of all frames. A similar worry runs through Hannah Arendt's book *The Human Condition* (Arendt 1958). Arendt too attempts to work out some of the implications of the emergence of the possibility that the earth can be seen as if from out there, as a found not made context of all human activity, hopes and ambitions.

Arendt begins her book with a discussion of the first satellite, which was sent into space in 1957. Like Heidegger might have done (and of course did do with the pictures from the moon), Arendt sees the satellite as a representation of an ability humanity has gained to upset the time-honoured order of things. Arendt suggests that the satellite is important because it heralds the dawn of a new age in which humanity can take steps towards escaping from the earth (to this extent then, perhaps it can be suggested that Hannah Arendt rather anticipated Heidegger's later sense of homesickness). What the science fiction writers would applaud, Arendt sees as a cause of great concern. Again like Heidegger, Arendt is worried about whether it is actually possible to make any kind of meaning out of the new capacities of technology and whether they imply a wholly new moment in the meanings of what it is to be human. Arendt asks and desperately tries to work out if the modern age which is represented in the practice and attempt practically to realize the ideals of emancipation and secularization, the modern age which began with a turning away from God, will 'end with an even more fateful repudiation of an Earth who was the Mother of all living creatures under the sky' (Arendt 1958: 2) And again like Heidegger, Arendt identifies the only hopes for any answers in the activity of thinking (she does not want to play a role in the preparation of humanity for the arrival of the God who will almost certainly never come). What Arendt advocates 'therefore, is very simple: it is nothing more than to think what we are doing' (Arendt 1958: 6). But that simplicity resides only in the saying; it is far from simple in the doing.

Unlike Heidegger, who mentions only the implications of the

movement into outer space, Arendt sees the movement out to space as but one moment in a much longer history of exploration. The effect of exploration has been that 'man [has] taken full possession of his mortal dwelling place and gathered the infinite horizons . . . into a globe whose majestic outlines and detailed surface he knows as he knows the lines in the palm of his hand' (Arendt 1958: 226–227).

For Arendt, as the earth has become more and more known (so that it is increasingly contained within the palm of our hand), so it has become more and more small: 'Precisely when the immensity of available space on earth was discovered, the famous shrinkage of the globe began, until in our world . . . each man is as much an inhabitant of the earth as he is an inhabitant of his country' (Arendt 1958: 227). According to Arendt, the world has become smaller to the extent that distances have been shortened thanks to the increasing speed of the means of exploration, travel and communication: 'Speed has conquered space . . . it has made distance meaningless, for no significant part of a human life – years, months, or even weeks – is any longer necessary to reach any point on earth' (Arendt 1958: 227). Consequently, whereas his parents could send Charles Baudelaire on a voyage to India on the assumption that the journey not the arriving would make him a more conventional paragon of bourgeois virtue, for us the voyage is simply the boring interlude between departure and arrival. Speed means that unlike Baudelaire we do not change with the scenery; we change simply by virtue of our 'being there'.

Arendt only alludes to some of the technologies of speed and of the overcoming of the problem of distance. She only quickly refers to the fact that we (a constituency which for Arendt 'though the result of the modern age, is by no means identical with the modern age's world'; Arendt 1958: 227) have 'Brought the globe into our living rooms to be touched by our hands and swirled before our eyes' (Arendt 1958: 228). This is an elliptical reference to the role which the media have played in the reduction of the horizons of the earth into the size of the inside of a hand. The earth is something which we can all see everyday in so far as we have access to a television set. To this extent then perhaps Arendt adds another aspect to the fears which beset Martin Heidegger. She is adding the ingredient that, for us, the earth is likely to be completely and utterly uninteresting if it is taken for itself; it is perhaps something we look at without caring terribly much about it (either that or the earth has become little more than a symbol in what are sometimes somewhat simplistic advertising campaigns by environmentalist groups. By this token it can be speculated that environmental politics would be impossible without the photographs of the earth from the moon).

It is as if Hannah Arendt is aware of the dark side which is too frequently omitted from the celebrations of the Global Village. Arendt knows that in villages we might all be neighbours but in villages we also all might be prisoners who are prevented from escape by our neighbours when they become our gaolers (for one rather early depiction of what it is like to be a prisoner of the Global Village, see Zweig 1943). For Hannah Arendt, the earth is something which is known and understood to the extent that it is surveyed. The collapse of the boundaries of time and space consequent upon the increasing speed of movement means that the surveying capacity has become tighter and tighter and the earth has closed in upon its inhabitants. Building on Arendt's argument, it can be proposed that there is nowhere for us to go to if we wish to escape the spying and intrusions of the Global Village.

Nowhere except into the skies. Arendt places great importance upon the fact that the ability to survey the earth, and the ability to adopt the attitude of the surveyor in relation to the earth and its inhabitants, was given a quantum leap by the emergence of the technological ability to move into the skies and thus look at the earth as something down there and not something here, all around. Arendt argues that 'the human surveying capacity . . . can function only if man disentangles himself from all involvement in and concern with the close at hand and withdraws himself to a distance from everything near him' (Arendt 1958: 228). (Undoubtedly, Arendt is using the word disentanglement in at least two senses; it is about physical and moral distance.) Flight represents this process of disentanglement and pushes it to previously unimagined horizons. George Orwell intimated one of the aspects of this disentanglement when he wrote his pamphlet 'The Lion and the Unicorn'; he wrote as 'highly civilized human beings are flying overhead, trying to kill me' (Orwell 1984: 144).

Arendt comments that 'the decisive shrinkage of the earth was the consequence of the invention of the airplane, that is, of leaving the surface of earth altogether'. The message of this observation is that the airplane can be taken to stand 'like a symbol of the general phenomenon that any decrease of terrestrial distance can be won only at the price of putting a decisive distance between man and earth, of alienating man from his immediate earthly surroundings' (Arendt 1958: 228). Here, the two meanings of disentanglement become quite clear.

This earth alienation is rooted intellectually in the conceit of the natural sciences that through their methodology they possess the Archimedean point of all observation and, therefore, of all knowledge. Arendt argues that the line and mode of enquiry set in train by Copernicus established that human sensual observations of the world could not be relied upon to be the source of truth because they are capable of being deceived. Quite simply, from the point of view of the individual looking at the skies it is quite possible to contend that the sun moves around the earth. But Copernican science proved that the contrary is in fact the case. Consequently, the telescope can be taken to stand as a technology of the alienation of humanity from the earth; instead of concerning itself only with the earth and direct human apprehensions of it, humanity began to employ technologies in order to operate on the field of the universe. According to Arendt, this movement 'was in fact an indication of the astounding human capacity to think in terms of the universe while remaining on the earth'. It was also an indication of 'the perhaps even more astounding human ability to use cosmic laws as guiding principles for terrestrial action' (Arendt 1958: 240).

These are some of the things which the phrase 'earth alienation' implies; humanity was taken beyond the earth and instead possessed of the ability to see the earth as simply one place amongst others, as one place which, if correctly understood, could be seen to obey laws which existed independently of it. Descartes added a new twist to this earth alienation when he proposed that true knowledge can only be acquired when the mind is free to play with formulas of its own construction. In other words, Cartesian methodology implies that even though the earth is made a constituent part of a universe, the universe itself is subordinated to the operation and solutions of a mathematics which is itself only possible because of the ability of the human mind to conjure up and think in terms of formulas and symbols. Much as with the simultaneous establishment of the *cogito* as the basis of all certain truth about the individual, Descartes' mathematical formulae were taken to be able to gain access to a more true and eternal knowledge than that which could be gained from empirical observations alone. Man becomes the master-surveyor of the universe, a surveyor who can know the truth of everything even if he cannot see it all: 'mathematics succeeded in reducing and translating all that man is not into patterns which are identical with human, mental structures' (Arendt 1958: 242).

Copernican science makes the telescope the Archimedean point of the truth of the universe. Cartesian doubt reduces the universe to mathematical formulae which are generated in the mind. Descartes chose 'as ultimate point of reference the pattern of the human mind itself, which assures itself of reality and certainty within a framework of mathematical formulas which are its own products' (Arendt 1958: 258). Thus Descartes gives humanity the ability to survey everything everywhere to the extent that everything can be reduced to a handful of numbers and symbols. Humanity gains power and control only to the extent that alienation goes ever deeper, ever further. And Descartes' move can be identified as the point of the emergence of the processes which, for Arendt, eventually result in the sending of satellites into space: 'Prior to the shrinkage of space and the abolition of distance through railroads, steamships, and airplanes, there is the infinitely greater and more effective shrinkage which comes about through the surveying capacity of the human mind'. The mind through the 'use of numbers, symbols, and models can condense and scale earthly physical distance down to the size of the human body's natural sense and understanding' (Arendt 1958: 227).

But if the human mind has become the Archimedean point from which all the universe can be surveyed, and from which all truth can be known irrespective of appearances, then that mind has not itself remained immune from the impact of processes and arrangements which Arendt needs to emphasize. For Arendt, the earth alienation which surveying requires and exacerbates has something approaching a counterpart in the alienation of the individual from the world. She talks about both earth alienation (which is represented in the attitude of disentangled surveying) and world alienation (the attitude of the individual in relation to the world which is the condition and situation of her or his existence). Indeed, Arendt proposes that: 'World alienation, and not self-alienation as Marx thought, has been the hallmark of the modern age' (Arendt 1958: 231).

Arendt's notion of world alienation is heavily indebted to Max

Weber's discussion of inner-worldly asceticism. In an immensely Weberian manner Arendt defines world alienation as an attitude in which 'enormous, strictly mundane activity is possible without any care for or enjoyment of the world whatever, an activity whose deepest motivation, on the contrary, is worry and care about the self' (Arendt 1958: 230–231). Arendt's objection to Marx is, then, that the modern world actually pays a great deal of attention to the self. Against Marx (or at least against her reading of Marx), Arendt contends that the inhabitants of the modern world tend to have themselves as the central problem of life. The inhabitants of the modern world are not alienated from themselves if only because they experience and confront themselves as a considerable problem and difficulty to overcome. They pay themselves too much attention to ever become alienated. The denizens of the modern world tend to elevate their selves to the highest possible status and pay the world around them hardly any attention at all. Put another way, it might be said that in the situation of world alienation, we are all like Puritans.

The paradox of the profound care of the self associated with the stance of inner-worldly asceticism is quite clear from Weber. This asceticism is identified by Weber as having its roots (in so far as they are relevant to his study of the spirit of capitalism) in the Protestant notion of the calling. According to the notion of calling some individuals are pre-ordained to attain heaven. However, it is impossible for us to know beforehand whether we have been called or not. There is nothing the individual can do about this situation except accept God's will in good grace and assume that one is a member of the elect. Consequently, every individual is motivated to work hard in this world on the basis of a wager that if they do not they will lose the place reserved for them beside God. On the one hand this argument makes the sensuous world which surrounds us little more than a devilish distraction to divert us from our God-given duties: 'this asceticism turned with all its force against one thing: the spontaneous enjoyment of life and all it had to offer' (Weber 1930: 166). On the other hand it involves a central concern with the self: the notion of the calling was 'for the individual an incentive methodically to supervise his own state of grace in his own conduct, and thus to penetrate it with asceticism' involving 'a rational planning of the whole of one's life in accordance with God's will' (Weber 1930: 153).

According to Weber, in its relationship with the world of

material artifacts-become-distractions, inner-worldly asceticism made the individual into little more than a servant to things. Since God had given things to the individual, so the individual had a duty to defend and nurture them; a duty to possess them and acquire ever more in order to glory God. But of course the greater the glory to God the greater the temptation to lapse into enjoyment of the pleasures of the here and now. Hence the self must be ever self-vigilant. Weber comments that: 'The idea of a man's duty to his possessions, to which he subordinates himself as an obedient steward, or even as an acquisitive machine, bears with chilling weight on his life.' He continues: 'The greater the possessions the heavier, if the ascetic attitude toward life stands the test, the feeling of responsibility for them, for holding them undiminished for the glory of God and increasing them by restless effort' (Weber 1930: 170). Weber contends that to the extent that this series of beliefs underpins a spirit of capitalism so it has taken a hold on everyone who is required to live and work in capitalist arrangements. The attitude towards the world and work which was a cloak on the shoulder of the Puritan saint has been transformed into something much weightier and harder to bear as it has spread out. As Weber famously puts it: 'fate decreed that the cloak should become an iron cage' (Weber 1930: 181).

Hannah Arendt refuses to speculate on why and how earth alienation and world alienation could emerge at more or less the same time. After all, the development of any kind of account which could explain such a coincidence would cause her to posit precisely the kind of a philosophy of history which her statement that 'history is a story of events and not of forces or ideas with predictable courses' explicitly disavows (Arendt 1958: 229). (For an extremely helpful discussion of Arendt's refusal to buy into a philosophy of history, see Fehér 1987.) All Arendt can say about the virtual simultaneity of earth alienation and world alienation is that it 'may be one of the many coincidences that make it so difficult for the historian not to believe in ghosts, demons, and *Zeitgeists*.' Arendt simply notes that the two alienations emerged together even though: 'What is so striking and disturbing is the similarity in utmost divergence.' She continues to make it plain that the Weberian 'innerworldly alienation has nothing to do, either in intent or content, with the alienation from the earth inherent in the discovery and taking possession of the earth' (Arendt 1958: 228). But together they comprise a specifically modern

12

attitude: 'while world alienation determined the course and the development of modern society, earth alienation became and has remained the hallmark of modern science' (Arendt 1958: 240).

Whatever the explanation of their coincidence and development, the two different relationships of alienation have the implication of making the earth and the world simple things to be used (and of course the attitude of using itself embodies an assumption that in relation to the subjective user the used stands as an objective out there; as something very much like the standing reserve as it is understood by Martin Heidegger). Relationships to the earth and the world become structured around attitudes and practices of productivity and creativity. The emergence of productivity and creativity as organizing principles of social and cultural activity is important because, according to Arendt, it implies the establishment of a single definition of what it is and what it means to be human. Arendt writes that: 'Productivity and creativity, which were to become the highest ideals and even the idols of the modern age in its initial stages, are inherent standards of *homo faber*' (Arendt 1958: 269). In other words, these standards imply and establish a definition of human being in which humanity is understood as a worker, as a maker.

Arendt defines *homo faber* as the toolmaker who has an exclusively instrumental attitude towards the objects which surround him: 'It is "for the sake of" usefulness in general that *homo faber* judges and does everything in terms of "in order to"' (Arendt 1958: 134). In other words, *homo faber* is incapable of distinguishing between means and ends. In so far as the activity of *homo faber* is founded on the terrain of the processes of productivity and creativity which can never be consummated (because they are means to an end which by definition can never be achieved), so actually there is no distinction to be made between means and ends. Everything is a means in itself; a means to some end which will probably arrive the day after tomorrow.

For *homo faber*, the main questions to ask of anything are 'How?' and 'Why?' These are important questions. On the one hand they imply that *homo faber* identifies the milieu of things waiting to be used as standing out there; *homo faber* has no relationship with those things (he is disentangled from them) except in so far as they are of concern to productivity and creativity. What the eye surveys, the hand turns into something new. In both of these ways then (by both mind and hand) *homo faber* manages to appro-

13

priate the earth and the world and demonstrate, through his very ability to transform them, his alienation from earth and world alike. But on the other hand the questions 'How?' and 'Why?' imply an understanding of the universe in terms of mutability, change and process rather than in terms of the identification of discrete things which are taken to remain the same for all time.

For Arendt this concentration on process is of utmost importance. It means that humanity can be about some things but not others: 'In the place of the concept of Being we now find the concept of Process.' Arendt continues to draw out some of the consequences of this shift in emphasis, away from the belief in some truth which is to be revealed but which in itself remains invariant and towards another standard of truth which is invisible as such and only manifest in certain products: 'whereas it is in the nature of Being to appear and thus disclose itself, it is in the nature of Process to remain invisible, to be something whose existence can only be inferred from the presence of certain phenomena' (Arendt 1958: 270). As such, process itself is understood to be something which goes on and exists beneath and beyond surface appearances. The process itself can only be known by a surveyor who is able to adopt the posture of the Archimedean point in relation to that which is surveyed.

The world-view of *homo faber* is consequently quite mechanistic. In this order of things the process of making becomes all important; the things made are themselves little more than by-products on some journey which is accorded a much greater significance. The thing which is made is accorded little or absolutely no privilege in and of itself. Indeed, for *homo faber*, things are a very definite obstacle to overcome. Indeed, 'from the standpoint of *homo faber*, it was as though the means, the production process or development, was more important than the end, the finished product' (Arendt 1958: 270–271). Furthermore: 'Under modern conditions, not destruction but conservation spells ruin because the very durability of conserved objects is the greatest impediment to the turnover process, whose constant gain in speed is the only constancy left wherever it has taken hold' (Arendt 1958: 229–230). What Hannah Arendt is concerned about is what it means to be human in this situation of constant and perpetual change, this situation of process in which there is nothing definite which might be able to constitute any kind of compass point or safe haven for humanity in the universe.

Homo faber is a figure who operates in terms of processes of perpetual change and transformation. For Arendt this operation represents nothing other than a serious qualification of what it means to be human in the world. Arendt provides something by way of a catalogue of the world-view of *homo faber*. It is characterized by: an instrumentalization of the world and the adoption of a purely instrumental relationship to it; 'confidence in tools and in the productivity of the maker of artificial objects'; faith in the applicability of means–ends calculations to all problems everywhere; 'conviction that every issue can be solved and every human motivation reduced to the principle of utility'; a belief in sovereignty in relation to materially existing nature which is identified as something waiting to be used at will; the 'equation of intelligence with ingenuity' and a consequent contempt for all thought which cannot be seen to have an immediate practical value; a 'matter-of-course identification of fabrication with action'. (This catalogue and the quotations in it are provided in Arendt 1958: 279.)

For *homo faber* things are objective obstacles to be overcome in the ceaseless round of production and creativity. But Arendt claims that in fact things – objects – represent the measure of the extent to which humanity has been able to dwell in the world. As Arendt puts the matter: 'The task and potential greatness of mortals lies in their ability to produce things – works and deeds and words – which would deserve to be and, at least to a degree, are at home in everlastingness.' Through these objects which humanity has made, 'mortals could find their place in a cosmos where everything is immortal except themselves. By their capacity for the immortal deed . . . men . . . attain an immortality of their own and prove themselves to be of a "divine" nature' (Arendt 1958: 19). These are very great claims to make for the human ability to make objective things. And so the stakes of the tendency of *homo faber* to relegate things to process are equally great; the tendency implies that humanity ceases to be able to prise itself apart from the animal and from the futility of utter mortality. *Homo faber* might well herald the death of humanity.

Arendt bewails the rise of *homo faber* because, for her, it implies an unprecedented and undesirable rearticulation of the human condition. *Homo faber* identifies the process of work as the single truth of what it is to be human. However, for Arendt the human condition should be, and demands to be, characterized by a far

15

more complex conception of human qualities, capacities and ambitions. This conception is explained in her notion of the *vita activa*. For Arendt, the *vita activa* has three component parts; labour, work and action. These three activities are of fundamental importance because: 'each corresponds to one of the basic conditions under which life on earth has been given to man' (Arendt 1958: 9).

The activity of labour 'corresponds to the biological process of the human body, whose spontaneous growth, metabolism and eventual decay are bound to the vital necessities produced and fed into the life process by labour'. Consequently, and as Arendt puts it: 'The human condition of labor is life itself' (Arendt 1958: 9). Labour is about bodies and the satisfaction of their physical needs.

The activity of work refers to the human ability and need to make objects which can themselves be used as tools in an attempt to make some kind of meaning out of the exclusively human knowledge of individual mortality (according to Borges it is our knowledge that we will all die which distinguishes us from the rest of nature which has no such premonition of mortality). Arendt writes that: 'Work is the activity which corresponds to the unnaturalness of human existence, which is not embedded in, and whose mortality is not compensated by, the species' ever-recurring life cycle.' Indeed, thanks to the activity of work and its production of objective things 'each individual life is housed, while this world itself is meant to outlast and transcend them all' (Arendt 1958: 9). (In the light of this comment, Heidegger's fears because of the pictures from the moon might be due to a realization that each individual is housed in a built structure which might be about to fall apart at any moment.)

If labour and work refer to what might be called a politics of mortality, a politics which 'departs from the most banal "fact" of the human condition: we are all mortals and we are acutely aware of our limitedness in all our doings' (Heller and Fehér 1988: 103), then action, the third aspect of the *vita activa* refers to what might be seen as politics *per se*. Action is a relationship between individuals and not, like labour, a relationship with matter nor, like work, a relationship with things. Action 'corresponds to the human condition of plurality, to the fact that men, not Man, live on the earth and inhabit the world' (Arendt 1958: 9). Action is the expression of the fact that a plurality of human beings live in the world together and have to make sense of their being together. Action is required if a specifically reciprocal existence is going to be possible; action is the making of that possibility.

It is the coming together of these three aspects of the human condition which constitutes the *vita activa* and, in a dialectical twist: 'The world in which the *vita activa* spends itself consists of things produced by human activities; but the things that owe their existence exclusively to men nevertheless constantly condition the human makers' (Arendt 1958: 11). Arendt continues to explain that: 'The objectivity of the world – its object- or thing-character – and the human condition supplement each other.' Arendt continues to explain that this is because 'human existence is conditioned existence, it would be impossible without things, and things would be a heap of unrelated articles, a non-world, if they were not the conditioners of human existence' (Arendt 1958: 11). Or again: 'Things and men form the environment for each man's activities, which would be pointless without such location' (Arendt 1958: 23).

However, this general truth cannot be known from within the *vita activa* itself. Arendt's position seems to be that each of the three aspects of the *vita activa* can only really know of itself; left to itself and taken wholly in isolation each aspect would contain a tendency towards the reduction of the entire human condition to its own exclusive concerns and problems. Consequently, the overall conception of the *vita activa* has to have its foundations elsewhere. That elsewhere is identified by Hannah Arendt as the *vita contemplativa*. Indeed, 'the term *vita activa* receives its meaning from the *vita contemplativa*; its very restricted dignity is bestowed upon it because it serves the needs and wants of contemplation in a living body' (Arendt 1958: 16). In other words, the *vita contemplativa* may be defined as the thinking of the *vita activa*, a thinking which, however, the *vita activa* makes possible and nourishes precisely to the extent that it provides the material comforts which nourish the thinking body and precisely to the extent that it makes the objective things in terms of which thinking is possible.

Arendt identifies the *vita contemplativa* as heir to a tradition which has its origins in the thought of Aristotle, Augustine and Aquinas. In this tradition, the *vita activa* was identified as 'all kinds of active engagement in the things of this world' (Arendt 1958: 15) and, by contrast, the *vita contemplativa* was identified as

17

the only way of life which was free of any involvement with material needs and wants. As such, the *vita contemplativa* was established as distinct from the mundane world of labour and work; it came to stand in contrast to activity. The *vita contemplativa* established its legitimacy and authority by the claim that because it stood apart from the *vita activa* it was therefore and thereby capable of discovering the single truth of it. Its authority is based on 'the assumption that the same central human preoccupation must prevail in all activities of men, since without one comprehensive principle no order could be established' (Arendt 1958: 17). Such a position traditionally leads to a hierarchical conception of the human condition with the *vita contemplativa* at its very summit.

Arendt seems to be both seduced and troubled by this hierarchical conception. She is seduced because the hierarchy places thought and especially a politics which recognizes the plurality of humanity at the very pinnacle of human being in the world. Humanity thus demonstrates its exclusive humanity all the more it indulges in activities and relationships which stand apart from the compulsions of labour and work. The *vita contemplativa* stands as the organized expression of all of these activities and modes of making which are purely human. She is troubled by the hierarchy because it can be taken to imply that actually humanity should not be plural but that, in fact, humanity is only expressed in the *vita contemplativa* which seeks to discover the single organizing principle of all existence and being. If the *vita contemplativa* is made the summit of a hierarchy then all activities and all humans who do not participate in it are either servants to the masters, or fools to be re-educated, or a mob to be kept firmly at arms length. In any of these cases the plurality of human beings cannot at all be respected or represented in action. It is for these reasons that Arendt clings to the *vita contemplativa* while refusing to accept that it has some privileged insight on some privileged and all-inclusive standard of the absolute truth. Arendt contends that the engagement of the *vita activa* and the thinking of the *vita contemplativa* do not stand one beneath the other but, instead, 'might correspond to two altogether different central human concerns' (Arendt 1958: 18). Only in this way can the presence of differences and of others be accepted and built upon not just destroyed.

The reduction of the human condition to work and the identification of humanity as *homo faber* stands as a serious challenge to the possibility of the *vita contemplativa* and, therefore, to a recognition of the essential plurality of humanity. *Homo faber* cannot possibly recognize that: 'Plurality is the condition of human action because we are all the same, that is, human, in such a way that nobody is ever the same as anyone else who ever lived, lives, or will live' (Arendt 1958: 10). Instead, all *homo faber* emphasizes is work; the making of transient things which are held to be less significant than the ongoing process of the making. Certainly the productions of *homo faber* can offer to build a home for humanity in the world, but the building is of such a sort that fairly soon the home will either fall down or have to be demolished to make way for a new and improved version. Each individual life is housed in a world which actually might not outlast it. *Homo faber* consequently stands in a thoroughly ambivalent relationship to the *vita activa*. On the one hand, *homo faber* cannot possibly take account of the complexity and plurality of the human condition. Yet, on the other hand, *homo faber* continues to play on the terrain of the *vita activa* even though the terrain has been tilted and skewed almost beyond recognition.

But at least *homo faber* continues to play on the ground of the *vita activa*, however one-sided the field might have become. Even though Arendt is immensely concerned about the status of the human condition in a context when *homo faber* reigns supreme, what concerns her even more is what she sees as the distinct possibility that *homo faber* is also under attack to such an extent that even this reduction of the human condition might come to look quite reasonable in the light of what is about to follow; the reduction of humanity and the human condition to the activity of *animal laborans*. (Here it is possible to see how Arendt continues to cling to some notion of hierarchy in the *vita activa* and *vita contemplativa*; she is concerned about the rise of *homo faber* because it prejudices acknowledgement of human plurality and instead emphasizes work alone; she is concerned about the rise of *animal laborans* because it prejudices the activity of work and instead emphasizes life alone – and life is not exclusive to the human condition, it is shared with all living creatures.)

Because *homo faber* understands objective things to be but the latest instalment of a more important ongoing process of productivity and creativity, then the things which are made are necessarily born into oblivion. Furthermore, in so far as the processes of productivity and creativity become increasingly important (and,

19

of course, increasingly associated with technologies) then the turn-over of things will accelerate. The objects, the things, we have now will be consigned to oblivion all the sooner thanks to the development of yet new 'better and improved' versions. Just like me, the things I use live and die: 'It is as though we had forced open the distinguishing boundaries which protected the world, the human artifice, from nature, the biological process which goes on in its very midst' (Arendt 1958: 110). The implication of this transformation of objective things into entities which follow an almost material life is that: 'The ideals of *homo faber*, the fabricator of the world . . . have been sacrificed to abundance, the ideal of the *animal laborans*' (Arendt 1958: 110).

This abundance is not a means to an end. It is taken to be a much more straightforward satisfaction of the needs of life. Values and understandings which have any degree of abstraction or generality about them hold no appeal for *animal laborans*. When considering Arendt's invocation of the figure of *animal laborans* it is extremely tempting to recall and rephrase Marx's dictum in the *Economic and Philosophic Manuscripts* that within capitalist relationships of production, man 'only feels himself freely active in his animal functions . . . and in his human functions he no longer feels himself to be anything but an animal. What is animal becomes human and what is human becomes animal' (Marx 1977: 66). *Animal laborans* is almost a prisoner of a world which is experienced and interpreted as just being here. The figure stands as a dull pragmatist who critiques and criticizes absolutely nothing because critique does nothing about the satisfaction of needs in the situation of abundance (critique plays on a rather different terrain than that).

In so far as *animal laborans* comes to dominate the human condition, so humanity becomes a slave to the rhythm of the machines: 'In this motion, the tools lose their instrumental character, and the clear distinction between man and his implements, as well as his ends, becomes blurred' (Arendt 1958: 127). It is this dehumanization implied by the figure of *animal laborans* that is the cause of Arendt's greatest concerns. For her: 'The question . . . is not so much whether we are the masters or the slaves of our machines.' Rather the question is 'whether machines still serve the world and its things, or if, on the contrary, they and the automatic motion of their processes, have begun to rule and even destroy world and things' (Arendt 1958: 132).

The story of the fate of the *vita activa* and *vita contemplativa* which Hannah Arendt tells has a very clear narrative. Arendt tells of what she holds to be the decline and fall of the possibility that the human condition might offer the chance of a specifically human existence which is able to achieve its wildest dreams. The incidents in the story surround moments in the disarticulation of the component parts of the *vita activa* and the successive emergence in a trajectory of decline of one of the component parts to the detriment of all others. Yet Arendt refuses to accept as inevitable the situation in which the human condition has become virtually deprived of its humanity. In the end, and despite other similarities between them, Arendt does not at all anticipate Martin Heidegger's forlorn and desperate preparation for the arrival of God. Neither does she give up the struggle for humanity and just accept the barbarism which is emerging all around. For her, the story she tells is so serious that mysticism or quietism are simply not legitimate responses to it. She wants to reconstitute the human condition and recover the plurality of humanity from the commands of 'the society of jobholders' which 'demands of its members a sheer automatic functioning, as though individual life had actually been submerged in the over-all life process of the species' (Arendt 1958: 294).

As such, what Arendt is calling for is a reassertion of the *vita contemplativa* which can think the unity and generality of the human condition whilst also paying due care and attention to the plurality of humanity. She is making a case for the practitioners of the *vita contemplativa* not only to put their own house in order (and refuse to accept the blind pragmatism of thought which *animal laborans* requires) but also for them to help create the space for a reconstitution of the fully rounded *vita activa*. In that way the world might be made fit for humanity. Arendt's argument is not a resignation to the human condition as it has been redefined by *animal laborans* triumphant, instead it is a call to put *animal laborans* – and for that matter *homo faber* – back into its proper place.

Arendt does not want to murder *animal laborans*. Rather, her case is that this aspect of the *vita activa* must not be allowed to kill the other aspects. Once again plurality is at the centre of the analysis. On the one hand this means a politics of and for humanity. On the other hand it means an intellectual acceptance of the plurality of humanity and a refusal to accept the claim (with which many orthodox sociologists would agree) that if we turn the Archimedean point against ourselves we might be able to discover the ultimate truth and exclusive authoritative articulation of the human condition. Arendt knows that we are entangled in what we write and that to deny that entanglement is to deny the humanity of ourselves and those we write about. As such, writing can be thinking can be acting.

Treated purely as a moral and political thesis, Hannah Arendt's account of the tribulations and possibilities of the *vita activa* is extremely compelling. Apart from her refusal to give up on the world as it has emerged, Arendt's emphasis on respect for the plurality of human existences is immensely apposite. It is indeed important to remember at all times that we live in a world of men and women and not of Man. It is largely for these moral and political reasons that I have paid so much attention to Arendt's work and tried to recount her position as appropriately as I can.

With Arendt's *The Human Condition*, as indeed with every other text I discuss in this book, I have adopted the strategy which Richard Rorty calls 'inspired reading'. Rorty contrasts the inspired reading of texts to the strategy of 'methodical reading'. The methodical reader attempts to discover the definitive and absolute truth of the text (an attempt which is doomed to failure; every reader will discover her or his own truth). The methodical reader rather tends to place the text under a glass dome in the museum. But, by contrast, the inspired reader approaches the text as something which might change her or his life. An inspired reading identifies a text as a stimulus to creative thought and even action. The text is approached as an opportunity to think anew, and not as something which is once confronted, once explored to exhaustion, once discarded because there is nothing left to find.

Methodical reading is a testament to the erudition of the reader. Inspired reading is a testament to the provocation of the text. As Rorty puts it, the inspired reader is concerned with, 'knowing what you want to get out of a person or thing or text in advance and hoping that the person or thing or text will help you want something different'. In other words, for the strategy of inspired reading the text is a partner in a ceaseless dialogue, a partner in an endless action on the terrain of plurality, a partner who is engaged with in the hope 'that he or she or it will help you change your life'. (The two quotations from Rorty are taken from

Zygmunt Bauman's review essay of a book by Gillian Rose; Bauman follows Rorty in commending inspired reading and his essay stands as an example of the strategy; Bauman 1993.) Such an approach to texts is not too far removed from the kind of reading strategy which Kurt Wolff advocates. Wolff suggests that the analyst should seek to establish a relationship with whatever it is that she or he is studying. In this way it is possible to use that which is being studied as an avenue and an opportunity for the development of an existentially meaningful truth. This truth is one which is located in dialogue; a dialogue between the subject and the object of enquiry, a dialogue between the writer and the reader, a dialogue between me and you and all the other writers who are discussed in this book. Through that dialogue it is possible to understand who and where we are. It is possible to understand the essence of our human situation in the here and now. Wolff makes a case for 'the neglected or abused approach of existential truth – neglected because considered unscientific; abused because thought to legitimate sentimentality and imprecision, and to replace scientific truth' (Wolff 1988: 716). (Here I have been summarizing some of the main points of Wolff's strategy of surrender and catch.) This book is written in terms of precisely that kind of existential approach.

This book takes Arendt as its point of departure. This book has been inspired by Arendt. And because it has been inspired it does not at all attempt to slavishly imitate her. In Wolff's terms I have sought to offer a relationship with Arendt and I have not at all attempted to provide any information about her or her book. That would make Arendt a museum exhibit. This book can be read as a journey from Arendt (and therefore because of Arendt; it is a journey which is grateful to Arendt) since whilst I agree with Arendt's account of what has happened to the *vita activa* I find it difficult to share her belief that with enough effort the *vita contemplativa* can be reconstituted such that a truly human condition might be able to emerge. I want to propose that contemporary social and cultural processes are such that any reconstitution of the *vita contemplativa*, and certainly any reconnection of it to the strands of the *vita activa* is highly improbable.

I do not doubt Arendt's hope because I wish to go further than Arendt went and propose that *animal laborans* has now become all that we can be. After all, if *animal laborans* is our fate it becomes difficult to explain how a book like this, or for that matter a book

like Arendt's own, could possibly be written, published and read.
I have two grounds for doubt about Arendt's faith. Putting these
doubts into somewhat speculative hypotheses it is possible to
make two proposals.

Firstly, it can be proposed that although the *vita activa* pre-
sumes a human condition of the making of the world, it is possible
that what Arendt calls world alienation and earth alienation have
developed to such an extent and have taken such a hold over
human desires and ambitions that either the environment around
us is confronted as utterly found and quite bereft of any sign of
the making, or 'inner worldly asceticism' has taken such a grip
and become so defining of all that humans are and can be that we
simply accept the world as it is and do not entertain any wish to
change it. In these terms it is possible that we have all become
rather like Dostoevskian writers of notes from the underground;
writers of notes who have devoted so much attention to the self
that it can only be despised, who have fled from a wider world
which is loathed, who can only achieve self-affirmation through
the howls which come with a tooth-ache (Dostoevsky 1974). Or it
is possible that we might all have become like Weber's specialists
without spirits and sensualists without heart (Weber 1930: 182).

Secondly, it can be proposed that whereas Arendt stresses the
point that the *vita contemplativa* stands as the opposite to the *vita
activa*, social and cultural processes might mean that such an
opposition has become quite untenable. Arendt makes it plain
that the *vita contemplativa* has at least some of its roots in the
attempt by Aristotle to draw a distinction between 'quiet and
unquiet, between an almost breathless abstention from external
physical movement and activity of every kind' (Arendt 1958: 15).
For Arendt this distinction means that the *vita contemplativa* constructs the *vita activa* 'from the viewpoint of the absolute quiet of
contemplation' (Arendt 1958: 15). Now it could well be that
Aristotle and Arendt see quiet as a metaphorical more than an
environmental condition. But even if this is the case, the metaphor does imply some kind of existential situation of silence and
repose in contrast to sound and fury; contemplation stands apart
from the noise of the world. However, contemporary social and
cultural relationships, and of course contemporary technologies,
are extremely noisy (and if Arendt and Aristotle do mean quiet to
be a metaphor alone, it is perfectly possible to see the contention
that contemporary relationships and technologies are noisy as a

metaphor also). It can be speculated that the noisiness of this world means that the silence and the quiet required by contemplation is actually impossible to find. It is possible that the contemporary environment is so terribly noisy (so unquiet) that any contemplation of it is impossible because, in fact, all of our critical and sensual capacities are absolutely stunned.

This book seeks to explore these speculative hypotheses. In that way it will be possible to examine whether it is likely that the *vita activa* and the *vita contemplativa* might be reconstituted; whether it is possible that the human condition might be rearticulated so that it is better able to reflect the plurality of humanity; whether social and cultural relationships have consigned humanity to a fate of the dull acceptance of what exists and a pragmatic adaption to it. In a sentence this book seeks to explore the condition of humanity in this world which has been so well made that all trace of the making has been quite effaced.

2

FINDING

Hannah Arendt places a very great emphasis upon the argument that the human condition is importantly constituted in the human ability to make things. For her, humanity is a constituency which expresses its humanity as a quality in so far as it is able to build its own objective world. The fabrication of objects is at once the expression of human being (it is the product of the conditions of labour and work) and the means by which human being can be constructed and identified as distinctive in the otherwise all too similar mêlée of material and organic things.

The objective world is represented in material artifacts which stand as a barrier between the properly human and the properly natural milieux. The human condition consequently requires human artifice if it is to be indubitably human. (To put all of this into a somewhat simplistic formula, it can be said that for Arendt human fabrication involves the making of human freedom; in these terms freedom is both ontological and practical. It is not primarily ideational.) These objects – these things – are constructed by humanity in the guise of *homo faber* who works with and upon materials and 'fabricates the sheer unending variety of things whose sum total constitutes the human artifice' (Arendt 1958: 119). Here then the phrase 'human artifice' is to be understood very broadly. It refers to the entirety of human productions and, therefore, to the human production of distinguishable humanity. Indeed, these fabrications by *homo faber* 'give the human artifice the stability and solidity without which it could not be relied upon to house the unstable and mortal creature which is man' (Arendt 1958: 119). Fabrication means that humanity can go on being human even though individual human beings come and go in the cycle of material birth and demise.

26

Arendt argues that these fabrications are able to constitute a stable home for the fundamentally unstable humanity because they are durable over time. The durability of what Hannah Arendt terms the human artifice has two linked aspects. Firstly, the human artifice is durable because even though single things might be used up and consumed nevertheless in principle they are replaceable: 'all single things can be constantly replaced with the change of generations which come and inhabit the man-made world and go away' (Arendt 1958: 120). Secondly, and as a consequence of the first aspect of the durability of the human artifice, the objective things which are made by *homo faber* take on an existence independently of their makers. Arendt talks about durability over time lending things a 'relative independence from men who produced and used them' so that they come to possess a capacity to 'withstand, "stand against" and endure, at least for a time, the voracious needs and wants of their living makers and users' (Arendt 1958: 120). Objects go on; we die. They are inorganic and durable whereas we, as humans, share the fate of all organic beings.

Without the ability of things to come to stand against their makers, without the emergence of this situation in which 'against the subjectivity of men stands the objectivity of the man-made world rather than the sublime indifference of an untouched nature' (Arendt 1958: 120), humanity would be quite incapable of securing itself and its identity over time. Humanity would be fated to perpetual flux and a wholly insubstantial and untenable human condition which would perpetually experience the enormous fears which can be associated with the category of the sublime. (Admittedly, Arendt does not talk about the sublime, but it is not unreasonable to suggest that an awareness of this category is implicit in much of her interpretation of the stakes of the human fabrication of the distinction between humanity and nature. The problem Arendt is talking about is that without the fabrication of objects it would be impossible to identify any kind of an imaginative dividing line between the milieu of the human condition and the milieu of nature as such.)

Additionally then, without the durability of the human artifice and especially its emergent ability to become a seemingly independent and self-sufficient house for its one-time makers, it would be impossible for humanity to become objective in its dealings with the world it finds itself in. And if humanity cannot be objective about some things neither can it be subjective about others (once again the dividing lines and mechanisms would be too blurred). For Arendt there can be little doubt about the necessity of the human artifice which is able to 'protect' humanity from nature. It is necessary because: 'Only we who have erected the objectivity of a world of our own from what nature has given us . . . can look upon nature as something "objective".' Indeed: 'Without a world between men and nature, there is eternal movement, but no objectivity' (Arendt 1958: 120). This is tantamount to saying that without the world of things standing as a barrier between two different conditions (milieux) which for Arendt need to be kept apart, the possibility of a recognizably human condition is more than a little questionable.

All of this is to begin to explore the profound significance of reification to Arendt's analysis of the human condition. She is quite certain that 'Fabrication, the work of *homo faber*, consists in reification' (Arendt 1958: 122). Reification represents the concerns of work. Firstly, reification involves violence in relation to nature (and so the dividing line which Arendt is so concerned to draw between the human artifice and nature is basically one between the oppressor and the oppressed, the agent and the victim – more emotively perhaps between the rapist and the raped. Of course, these renditions of the implications of the dividing line between the human and the natural milieux are considerably outside the narrative and terms of Arendt herself.). Reification requires material to work on and 'Material is already a product of human hands which have removed it from its natural location' and in so doing have either killed a life-process or have interrupted a slower natural process 'as in the case of iron, stone, or marble torn out of the womb of the earth' (Arendt 1958: 122). Consequently: 'The element of violation and violence is present in all fabrication, and *homo faber*, the creator of the human artifice, has always been a destroyer of nature' (Arendt 1958: 122).

It is tempting to propose that it was these kinds of arguments which to some extent underpinned Martin Heidegger's worries when he saw the photographs of the earth. In these terms perhaps he saw two things. Firstly, perhaps he saw that the violence which reification involves in relation to nature can only go so far before humanity is confronted with the need to uproot itself from the earth. The photographs demonstrate that the material over which humanity as *homo faber* practises such violence is not, in fact, in endless supply. The earth is finite and so, therefore, is the chance of the human ability to fabricate and reify its own homes (unless of course humanity moves to another planet when this one has been exhausted; and so science fiction becomes a dystopia for the uprooted humanity of the future). Secondly, perhaps Heidegger saw that centuries of violence in relation to nature have not in fact resulted in the fabrication of any reification whatsoever which can be identified as a specifically human artifice. Perhaps for Heidegger (in so far as it is reasonable to speculate as I am doing that his concerns at least to some extent ran parallel to the concerns of Hannah Arendt) the photographs demonstrated the chance that it is actually extremely difficult to entertain the conceit that there is any kind of durable dividing line between human and natural milieux. Perhaps Heidegger came to realize that it is not confidence but desperation which lurks behind the kind of claim which Arendt makes so clearly that with reification humanity knocks God off His pedestal of omnipotence: 'human productivity was by definition bound to result in a Promethean revolt because it could erect a man-made world only after destroying part of God-created nature' (Arendt 1958: 122). The photographs imply that in that case humanity must be a very petty Prometheus indeed.

The Promethean revolt is replenished and reasserted because fabrication is always carried out in accordance with a plan and a design. Fabrication is an exercise in means–ends rationality wherein the violence towards nature is not futile. Instead the violence is closely tied to notions of usefulness and utility for the achievement of a goal (Arendt 1958: 123, 125). What Arendt is attempting to establish with this claim is the importance of the complex relationships of the *vita activa*. Arendt is taking great care not to reduce the entirety of the *vita activa* to the single sphere of work. She is proposing that whilst work is the condition of the fabrication and reification of the human artifice, work itself is always carried out in accordance with the demands of a plan or a design which is – or should be – the expression of the unity of the articulations of the *vita activa*. The plan is outside of work even though it impinges upon that activity.

The plan is a product of the *vita contemplativa*. Arendt is im-plicitly going some way towards a reassertion of the primacy of thinking to the human condition. As such she is quite sure that 'the image or model whose shape guides the fabrication process not only precedes it, but does not disappear with the finished product'. This product (this reified and fabricated thing), 'survives intact, present, as it were, to lend itself to an infinite continuation of fabrication' (Arendt 1958: 124). In relation to the fabrications which are almost eternal in relation to the fleeting presences of individual men and women, ideational models themselves seem to be eternal. Consequently, 'Alone with his image of the future product, *homo faber* is free to produce, and again facing alone the work of his hands, he is free to destroy' (Arendt 1958: 126). The model of the plan makes both production and destruction meaningful; it makes them precisely human.

Arendt obviously understands reification in terms of an ongoing activity which has a definite beginning and a definite end (although it is quite possible that the hour of the practical achievement of the end resides in the dawning of the tomorrow which will never come). Reification is thus a continual enterprise in the fabrication of the human condition and of the demarcation of the boundary line which enables the emergence and adoption of an objective attitude towards nature. Reification consequently represents a building of the human condition which is free from enchantment and which can be known to be an expression of the emancipation of the humanity which has imitated the revolt of Prometheus (even though the imitation might not have been as glorious as humanity would have itself believe).

Thanks to her identification of reification as an activity, Hannah Arendt is able to assert its centrality to the fabrication of a human artifice which will always require work and which will, therefore, always distinguish human freedom from natural compulsion (and by extension this image is able to play a crucial role in Arendt's condemnation of the growing predominance of *animal laborans*; *animal laborans* is an image of the domination of compulsion). For Arendt, reification is an activity which never ends, in which the project of the building of the artificial home for humanity can never be completed because there is always some new improvement to be made or some foundation which needs the addition of just a little more concrete: 'A true reification, in other words, in which the produced thing in its existence is secured once and for all, has never come to pass' because the existence of the fabricated thing (its existence both in terms of use and existential meaning), 'needs to be reproduced again and again in order to remain within the human world at all' (Arendt 1958: 122).

In all of these formulations Arendt tends to use the word reification in a very specific way so that it refers only to the activity of fabrication. She uses the word in such a way that reification can only be understood to the extent that it is associated with the chances of human freedom. But what Hannah Arendt rather tends to understate is the very distinct possibility that the word reification might refer to extremely different processes and relationships. And in those alternative situations it might indeed be the case that true reification might be achieved. Fabrications might cease to belong to what is experienced as the human world. Reification does not only mean the fabrication of concrete material objects; it also means the tendency of those material objects to stand not just apart from but also over and above their erstwhile creators. Reification can indeed mean the movement of fabrications outside of the human world so that relatively they stand like a second nature.

In his early book *The Theory of the Novel*, Lukács defined second nature on the basis of its difference to and from the first nature of the world which is experienced as self-sufficiently out there. He stresses the status of second nature as a human reification, the fabrication of which is forgotten or hidden away. According to Lukács, 'second nature is not dumb, sensuous and senseless like the first: it is a complex of senses – meanings – which has become rigid and strange, and which no longer awakens interiority'. Second nature becomes nothing other than 'a charnel-house of long-dead interiorities' (Lukács 1978: 64). That is to say, second nature no longer stands as a home built by humans for humans; it stands apart from them (us), as something as external as the sensuous yet senseless milieu of first nature. Second nature is a social and cultural fabrication from which individuals are alienated; they look at it and fail to see any sign of its human making.

Indeed, the emergence of second nature as something apart from its makers has profound implications for the social and cultural (my terminology, not Lukács's) apprehension of first nature. According to Lukács: 'Estrangement from nature (the first nature), the modern sentimental attitude to nature, is only a projection of man's experience of his self-made environment as a prison instead of as a parental home' (Lukács 1978: 64).

Furthermore, without the establishment of second nature out of human fabrication (an establishment which is founded upon a presumably temporal and existential 'sterile power of the merely existent'; Lukács 1978: 153), it is possible that first nature cannot be apprehended, imagined or experienced either: 'The first nature, nature as a set of laws for pure cognition, nature as the bringer of comfort to pure feeling, is nothing other than the historico-philosophical objectivation of man's alienation from his own constructs' (Lukács 1978: 64). This phrase implies two processes. Firstly, it implies that the non-human milieu becomes invested with human attributes and qualities because humanity quite fails to see itself in its own productions. Secondly, it implies that first nature can only be known through the extent to which it can be made to approximate to laws which are, in fact, quite external to it (a point which is broached in a slightly different way by Hannah Arendt).

However perhaps Lukács's most sustained analysis of the processes and implications of reification is to be found in *History and Class Consciousness* (Lukács 1971), a text which carries on a few of the themes contained in *The Theory of the Novel* yet wholly rebuilds them in terms of an attempt to construct an orthodox Marxism. In other words, whilst Lukács's categories of second nature and reification are similar to the extent that they represent attempts to grasp much the same processes, they are significantly different to the extent that, for Lukács at least, the category of reification is much more persuasive and solid than the category of second nature. *The Theory of the Novel* had been written in 1914–15, and by 1962 Lukács was arguing that the best thing to do with this earlier book is 'reject it root and branch' (Lukács 1978: 23).

In *History and Class Consciousness* Lukács does not identify fabrication as necessarily implicated in reification. Rather, he argues that reification is a consequence of specifically capitalist relationships of production. Consequently, Lukács does something which Hannah Arendt tends not to do. Whereas Arendt provides a broad and grand picture which operates on the terrain of ontology and epistemology (a terrain which sees the human condition in immensely large terms as applicable to all humans everywhere irrespective of the specific articulations of the human condition or specific situations of human being), Georg Lukács is rather more concerned to emphasize the organization of fabrication in capitalism. The problem with Lukács's account is, however, that his analysis of capitalist relationships is tied to a deeply teleological version of Marxism which takes the proletariat to be the agent which will be able to rehumanize the world of things and re-establish the equation between (in Arendt's terminology) fabrication and freedom. The problem reading Lukács is precisely one of attempting to rescue the account of reification from the faith in the revolutionary proletariat; the problem is precisely one of having to confront the possibility that if that faith is removed perhaps a great deal of the value of this part of Lukács's work tends to disappear along with it.

Lukács's analysis of reification (and his depiction of the second possible meaning of the word, the meaning which Arendt rather underexplores) is heavily indebted to Marx's account of commodity fetishism. Lukács writes that reification means that: 'a man's own activity, his own labour becomes something objective and independent of him, something that controls him by virtue of an autonomy alien to man' (Lukács 1971: 87). In the first part of that passage, Lukács is adopting a position which is similar to that of Arendt; like Arendt he is suggesting that reification involves the construction and the identification of an objective world of things. However, he quickly begins to move along a different path to Arendt when he stresses that these reifications do not simply constitute a world of objectivity which is experienced through objects but that they also come to stand apart from their makers to such an extent that they become alien to the relationships of their production.

A crucial aspect of that alienation is due to the tendency of reification to appear to obey natural and not social and cultural laws of development. Lukács identifies two strands of this tendency towards existence as if by nature. Firstly, Lukács suggests that through reification, 'a world of objects and relations between things springs into being'. In this world: 'The laws governing these objects are indeed gradually discovered by man, but even so they confront him as invisible forces that generate their own power' (Lukács 1971: 87). (The reference to the discovery of laws is quite interesting. Perhaps here Lukács and his translator have themselves fallen into the trap of accepting the conceit of existence as if by nature; one wonders if Lukács would not have been better served if he had spoken not of the discovery but of the invention of the laws of nature.) Secondly, and here Lukács's debt to Marx is even more stark than it is elsewhere, 'a man's activity becomes estranged from himself, it turns into a commodity which, subject to the non-human objectivity of the natural laws of society, must go its own way independently of man just like any other consumer article' (Lukács 1971: 87).

One profound and serious consequence of these relationships of reification is the impact they have on the consciousness of individuals (and here Lukács is taking up Marx's dictum that it is not the consciousness of individuals that determines their being but the conditions of their being which determine consciousness). To the extent that the productions and abilities of the individual are interpreted as subject to seemingly natural laws so, 'his qualities and abilities are no longer an organic part of his personality, they are things which he can "own" or "dispose of" like the various objects of the external world' (Lukács 1971: 100). Indeed, Lukács believes that: 'there is no natural form in which human relations can be cast, no way in which man can bring his physical and psychic "qualities" into play without their being subjected increasingly to this reifying process' (Lukács 1971: 100).

By paying attention to the two meanings of the word reification it is possible to identify an important cultural dialectic which plays around the status of nature as an artifice. This allusion to nature as artifice is indebted to the work of Agnes Heller (who is herself of course significantly influenced by Hannah Arendt and Georg Lukács alike). According to Heller, the understanding of nature as an artifice (as an artificial construction grounded in social and cultural attitudes towards and treatments of the earth) has the effect of establishing one standard or institutional arrangement as the only possible standard or arrangement by which a communal human life is possible. That single institution or arrangement comes to seem to exist by nature precisely because it seems to be universal and therefore applicable at all times and in all places. The natural artifice is essentially the conceit that there can be no social and cultural arrangements and relationships other than the arrangements and relationships which always already exist here and now.

Heller follows the Aristotelian claim 'that arrangements common to all political bodies and societies that are otherwise completely different in kind exist "by nature"' (Heller 1990: 146). In other words, nature is vested in, and vouched by, tradition. It is precisely the assumption that things cannot be other than they are which defines the conceit that they are established on the

terrain of immutable nature: 'Whatever is common to all socio-
political arrangements exists "by nature"' (Heller 1990: 145). Or
even whatever is simply taken to exist in common. This is even
though 'A virtually infinite variety of arrangements is possible
within the general mode of the natural artifice' (Heller 1990: 145).
However Heller contends that this conceit of nature is liable to
collapse 'when and where the "natural" appears as artificial; a
man-made construct that can be deconstructed' (Heller 1990: 145).
(Heller identifies this when and where with the emergence of
specifically modern imaginations and practices; with modernity.)

'The deconstruction of the "natural artifice" is believed to go
with the destruction of the whole of tradition: of all beliefs, con-
victions, certainties, morals, religions, meaningful ways of life'
(Heller 1990: 147). Heller suggests that even though such a belief
might be well placed, the moral lesson that conservative com-
mentators tend to draw from it might not be quite so justifiable.
For Heller, the deconstruction of the assumption that things are
simply the way things have to be actually represents the chance
for something like a drastic rehumanization of the world. Heller
admits that the deconstruction of natural artifice tends to uproot
traditions from their time-honoured moorings. It tends to
demolish the taken for grantedness of the usual ways of life. But:
'If one presupposes . . . that deconstruction is not destruction . . .
the fact that traditional ethical terms are free-floating, sometimes
out of context, does not forebode doom.' Instead it forebodes
'radical rearrangements of forms of human cooperation and the
mechanisms of problem-solving' (Heller 1990: 147).

Although Heller's discussion of the deconstruction of natural
artifice is very useful and even though it is able to lend some
support to Arendt's claim that the work of *homo faber* more or less
of necessity involves violence towards nature (a violence which is
for Arendt a real material actuality whereas for Heller it is intellectual as well) it is a little problematic. Firstly, it rather tends
to gloss over resistances and oppositions to the deconstruction of
natural artifice. Heller rather tends to create the impression that
the process of deconstruction was a relatively flat and straightforward affair which followed a single trajectory more or less
without deviation. Consequently Heller is happy to contend that
'The deconstruction of one element [of the natural artifice] was
followed by the deconstruction of several others with increasing
speed, until the aim of an alternative socio-political arrangement

appeared on the horizon' (Heller 1990: 146). Perhaps that sentence oversimplifies a difficult process. Secondly, and linked to the tendency towards the simplification of complex relationships, the way Heller talks about the deconstruction of natural artifice rather implies that once an act of deconstruction has been carried out it does not need to be carried out ever again. She rather tends to imply a once-and-never-to-be-needed-again deconstruction. If the first problem glosses social and cultural relationships, the second problem exempts the deconstruction of natural artifice from dialectical tensions. Yet it is precisely these tensions which must be borne in mind if the processes and relationships, and also the fates, of the human condition are to be examined.

I want to propose that instead of talking about natural artifice as a single category, the words nature and artifice should be separated from each other. In that way, a dialectical imagination can re-enter the frame. It is not just the case that nature is an artifice. The analysis of the two meanings of the word reification goes quite a considerable way towards demonstrating the distinct possibility that artifice can become like nature (artifice can become liable to experience as if it is natural). Heller herself admits this possibility that artifice might become like nature but, perhaps extremely surprisingly, she does not really pursue it. Heller merely references the possibility that the modernity which emerges out of the deconstruction of natural artifice might itself become nature if, firstly, it becomes shared by all existing cultures such that it is a property held in common and, secondly, if the modern imaginations and arrangements can 'generate the mechanisms for cultural-ethical reproduction, and, more importantly, human motives for this reproduction' (Heller 1990: 146). More than this she does not say.

The core of the seeming self-sufficiency which comes to surround fabrications is to be found in the ability of material things to have a longevity over time which the ideas and plans informing their making do not possess. Put another way, things remain long after the reasons for their existence have been forgotten; and so the material remnants of once great plans are present only in their complete and utter obsolescence. They are like fossils. And to the extent that they become like mute legacies from the past they imply a restriction of the possibilities and opportunities of human being. They become an obstacle to be overcome in the name of the fabrication by humans of a home for humans. These fossil things endure beyond their function and beyond their utility to such an extent that they exist as if they are natural.

Without doubt Walter Benjamin is the analyst *par excellence* of the fabrication which is reified and like a nature of the social and cultural construction. According to Adorno, Benjamin's work stands as a natural history of the social and cultural. Adorno believed that Benjamin was, 'drawn to the petrified, frozen or obsolete elements of civilization, to everything in it devoid of domestic vitality no less irresistibly than is the collector to fossils or to the plant in the herbarium' (Adorno 1967: 233). Building a lesson on the foundation of anecdote, Adorno went on to say of Benjamin that: 'Small glass balls containing a landscape upon which snow fell when shook were among his favourite objects. The French word for still-life, *nature morte*, could be written above the portals of his philosophical dungeons' (Adorno 1967: 233). These concerns of Benjamin were given something rather like their methodological and philosophical expression in the 'Theses on the Philosophy of History' which he wrote at the very end of his life. (The 'Theses' are contained in Benjamin 1973.)

According to Susan Buck-Morss, Benjamin's 'Theses' are structured around the contention that 'the myth of history as progressive change . . . needed dismantling' (Buck-Morss 1977: 168). She attributes Benjamin's belief in the redundancy of, and the obstacle to understanding the present represented by, the myth of history as progress to a recognition of the distinct possibility that 'a sense of historical destiny had lured people into the catastrophes of fascism and war' (Buck-Morss 1977: 168). (For illustrations and precise historical studies of how the myth could become such a lure if not trap, see Turner and Kasler 1992.) Undoubtedly, Buck-Morss is perfectly right to stress the relationship between Benjamin's meditations on the philosophy of history and the presence of the present he was experiencing (Benjamin was a writer who was profoundly disturbed by his time; he said 'No' to it). Such a sense of the tension between the claims of myth and the pressures of actuality does indeed run all the way through the 'Theses'. But it can be speculated that as much as he was trying to work out the tension between myth and actuality, Benjamin was also trying to propose an interpretation of history which might be able to take account of the two meanings of the word reification; of the dialectic of reification.

It is not at all far fetched to propose that one of the main themes which informs and underpins Walter Benjamin's 'Theses on the Philosophy of History' is precisely an effort to answer the question of how can history possibly be synonymous with or identical to a myth of progress if the fabrications which are meant to represent history increasingly come to stand outside of history. The objects which are the fruits of fabrication stand outside of history in so far as they are liable to emerge as second nature or reification. Benjamin's 'Theses' force a powerful realization that there might well be a distinctly nasty sting in the tail of the kind of claim made so strongly by Hannah Arendt that: 'The man-made world of things . . . becomes a home for mortal men, whose stability will endure and outlast the ever changing movement of their lives and actions.' Arendt herself saw cause to doubt this confident claim. She was not unaware of the possibility that the human artifice might not be able to transcend 'both the sheer functionalism of things produced for consumption and the sheer utility of objects produced for use' (Arendt 1958: 153).

But Benjamin saw the problem in much starker terms. Benjamin knew that the implicit progress which informs Arendt's claims might be untenable because things might well outlive their usefulness and thus come to stand apart from, and over and above, the human artifice thus restricting its opportunities and possibilities by their very senseless and meaningless material presence. For Arendt there is the possibility that things might be exhausted (although she quickly pushes the realization of the possibility to the back of her mind; when all is said and done she is too confident about the plenitude of fabrication). For Benjamin there is the more disturbing possibility that things might simply out live their usefulness and thus clutter up the world. And Benjamin's whole account of social and cultural relationships is built on the belief that just such a possibility has come to pass.

Benjamin's 'Theses' contain an attempt to shock the inhabitants of the present out of the obviousness and deadness of the reified fabrications which confront them (us). In so doing, Benjamin suggests, humanity will be redeemed from an experience of the present as the only way of life there can possibly be (an experience of the present as founded upon immutable natural laws) and instead humanity will receive the fullness of its past. Benjamin was concerned to explore the hypothesis that the past is not a procession which leads to the present nor an empty time which leads to the richness of today. Rather, Benjamin understood history as 'time filled by the presence of the now' (Benjamin 1973: 242–253). Such an argument makes 'the continuum of history explode' (Benjamin 1973: 253). And a writer such as Benjamin, 'A historical materialist . . . remains in control of his powers, man enough to blast open the continuum of history' (Benjamin 1973: 254). Benjamin is the bomb-maker.

Here, then, the preparedness to recognize the full past of humanity irrespective of the claims and conventions of the myth of progress offers the chance of a redemption from the conceit that this world is the only possible world (or rather the conceit that this world is the only world possible for us). This concern of Walter Benjamin tends to mirror the claim of T.S. Eliot that 'A people without history / Is not redeemed from time, for history is a pattern / Of timeless moments' (Eliot 1982: 145). In a not at all dissimilar vein Benjamin, in the third of the 'Theses', proposes that 'only for a redeemed mankind has its past become citable in all its moments' (Benjamin 1973: 246). (Of course, I am aware of the irony of identifying parallel themes in the work of Eliot and a writer like Benjamin who was so deeply indebted to the Jewish tradition.) In a dialectical twist, Benjamin is here arguing not just that reception to the past offers the chance of redemption from the present but, also, that only with redemption from the present can the past be recognized and accepted. For Benjamin then 'nothing that has ever happened should be regarded as lost for history' (Benjamin 1973: 246). (Benjamin's own homage to this contention is the massively unfinished – and unfinishable – 'Arcades Project'. For Benjamin's 'Arcades Project', see Benjamin 1983, Buck-Morss 1989.)

The claims made in Benjamin's Third Thesis are extended in the Fifth and Sixth Theses. In the Fifth Thesis, Benjamin attempts to add a little by way of detail to his commitment to the preparation for redemption from history. He makes it clear that any apprehension of history (which, to repeat, Benjamin does not understand as a continuum of progress or emptiness leading necessarily to the here and the now; Benjamin rather understands the past as a succession of moments of the now; the past as a series of presents) is premised on the presence of images of the past and the ability to make leaps of the imagination in the light of them. Benjamin's dependence on images only makes sense if it is assumed that these images are materialized in things. Consequently, Benjamin's method, as Adorno pointed out, is similar to the activity of the collector of fossils; without the reification of the image in things there would be no past about which images could possibly be imagined.

Benjamin writes that: 'The past can be seized only as an image which flashes up at the instant when it can be recognized and never seen again' (Benjamin 1973: 247). The historian-come-fossil-collector (come paleontologist of the reifications of human fabrications of the present; of the now) has to be prepared to accept all of these instantaneous flashes and lovingly catalogue them so that they will never be lost to the here and now. If they are lost, it is impossible for humanity to be redeemed from history: 'for every image of the past that is not recognized by the present as one of its own concerns threatens to disappear irretrievably' (Benjamin 1973: 247). With the death of the chance of redemption, so dies an aspect of the world that humanity has made for itself; so dies the chance that the world might ever be truly human again (again, that is, if it was ever truly human in the first place). Benjamin's aim is to rescue things-as-images from the fate of the death of reification.

Benjamin wants to rescue human fabrications from the destiny of becoming a world which is experienced and confronted as natural and not the product of deliberate and conscious artifice. As he put the matter in the Sixth Thesis: 'In every era the attempt must be made anew to wrest tradition away from a conformism that is about to overpower it' (Benjamin 1973: 247). Here the somewhat Messianic notion of redemption is made a little more concrete. The moment of redemption is prepared by a struggle against the dead weight of reification. For the Benjaminian historian of the presence of the past (and of the past of the present), all of this means that intellectual work must be carried out from the spaces of 'the "state of emergency" in which we live'. These states of emergency are 'not the exception but the rule'. For Benjamin, the exacerbation of a state of emergency, and the revelation of the presence of emergency through the past, is a way of resisting Fascism. It can lead to a freedom from the conceit that all the certainties about progress and rationality prove that Fascism either cannot happen or is little more than a temporary spasm in the death throes of capitalism. Benjamin's method is about standing in a state of emergency in relation to that kind of stupid certainty: 'The current amazement that the things we are experiencing are "still" possible in the twentieth century . . . is not the beginning of knowledge – unless it is the knowledge that the view of history which gives rise to it is untenable' (Benjamin 1973: 249).

The heart of the 'Theses on the Philosophy of History', as indeed the heart of Benjamin's whole approach, is to be found beating in the image of the Angelus Novus which he deploys in the Ninth Thesis. Benjamin takes his image from a painting by Paul Klee which, 'shows an angel looking as though he is about to move away from something he is fixedly contemplating. His eyes are staring, his mouth is open, his wings are spread.' According to Benjamin, this is how the Angel of History is conventionally pictured (Benjamin 1973: 249). The Angel of History looks to-wards the past and, famously: 'Where we perceive a chain of events, he sees one single catastrophe which keeps piling wreck-age upon wreckage and hurls it in front of his feet' (Benjamin 1973: 249). For Benjamin then, the Angel of History sees a past which consists in destruction and the smashing of things which would otherwise be whole. Indeed, Benjamin says that the Angel would like to stay in the present and make whole that which has been torn apart but he is being blown ever onwards: 'This storm irresistibly propels him into the future to which his back is turned, while the pile of debris before him grows skyward. This storm is what we call progress' (Benjamin 1973: 249).

Like most metaphors, Benjamin's reference to the Angel of History is at once highly suggestive and utterly obscure. However, some kind of sense can be made of it if the Ninth Thesis is read in the context of its companions. The figure of the Angel of History refers to the failed and ever-failing redemption which is associated with the myth of history as progress. Benjamin shows that progress is a process which goes ever onwards with-out being able to see precisely where it will come to rest (if it ever will or can come to rest; virtually by definition progress cannot stop). Progress can only be known to the extent that it represents a movement away from something. That movement itself can only be identified if attention is firmly focused on all of those things which were once players in the game of the fabrication of a home for humanity but which are turned into debris, into rubbish, by the ceaseless flight of progress. Progress means that fabrications come to get thrown away onto an ever-increasing pile of rubbish. The pile becomes more and more obvious whilst the individual things within it become increasingly indistinguishable from each other.

Benjamin's Angel of History is saying that any redemption is impossible all the time the myth of progress holds sway, all the time we are moving away from what we have made. But of course, that movement is utterly paradoxical. Thanks to progress the pile of debris grows greater and greater as more and more things are reduced to the status of obsolete rubbish. Yet precisely by virtue of that very process the pile remains long after any sense can be made of it. It is just there in all its obsolescence, standing as a dumb sign of how far we have come; there like a mountain which can only be contemplated or climbed.

Benjamin tries to respond to the flight of the Angel of History by struggling to stand outside of progress and by relying on the shocks which arise when it is realized that our rubbish was useful once upon a time. Consequently Benjamin is forced to realize that what we find useful will soon be obsolete. In this way, history (and especially therefore the history of reification through obsolescence) can be made to stop. The single moment can be turned into the remembering and therefore the redemption of all history: 'Where thinking suddenly stops in a configuration pregnant with tensions, it gives that configuration a shock, by which it crystallizes into a monad' (Benjamin 1973: 254). This monad is a mystic evaporation of reification become second nature: it stands as 'a Messianic cessation of happening, or, put differently, a revolutionary chance in the fight for the oppressed past' (Benjamin 1973: 254). Such a strategy enables Benjamin to proclaim that it is possible to rehumanize the past and reinterpret history irrespective of the demands of convention and dull taken-for-grantedness: 'As a result of this method the lifework is preserved in this work and at the same time cancelled; in the lifework, the era; and in the era, the entire course of history' (Benjamin 1973: 254).

What is clear from the 'Theses' is the extent to which Benjamin relies on things to crystallize the monad which makes it possible to 'blast a specific era out of the homogeneous course of history – blasting a specific life out of the era or a specific work out of the lifework' (Benjamin 1973: 254). Perhaps it is this tendency towards a dependency on pre-existing reified things which led to the most important aspects of Theodor Adorno's critique of Benjamin. Adorno knew that Benjamin wanted a redemption from history which would make it possible to 'scrutinize living things so that they present themselves as being ancient, "ur-historical" and abruptly release their significance' (Adorno 1967: 233). But for Adorno this meant that 'Benjamin's thought is so saturated with culture as its natural object that it swears loyalty to reification instead of flatly rejecting it.' Adorno saw in Benjamin a 'tendency to cede his intellectual power to objects diametrically opposed to it' (Adorno 1967: 233).

Adorno is implying that instead of revealing the mythic status and practical disasters of progress all Benjamin actually does is offer a counter-myth of things. Whereas in the myth of progress things become obsolete by continuing to exist long after they have ceased to be functional or useful, in Benjamin's counter-myth the very practical uselessness of things lends them an aura of mystery which indicates a way of preparation for redemption: 'everything, and especially the ephemeral, becomes in his own thought mythical . . . reconciliation is that of myth itself' (Adorno 1967: 233). These tendencies have their roots in Benjamin's debt to and fondness for Surrealism. Certainly Benjamin's attempts to extract a shock out of the crystallization of history in the monad bears a distinct similarity to some of the things that the Surrealists were trying to do.

According to Benjamin, the method of the Surrealists depends upon a strategy of 'profane illumination'. He sees this method receive its first outing in the work of André Breton. For Benjamin, Breton 'was the first to perceive the revolutionary energies that appear in the "out-moded"' (Benjamin 1989: 175). Benjamin went on to provide a list of the things which inspired the perception of the Surrealists. It is almost as if Benjamin is writing a quick resumé of the contents of his 'Arcades Project'. Benjamin catalogued the Surrealists' delight

> in the first iron constructions, the first factory buildings, the earliest photos, the objects that have begun to be extinct, grand pianos, the dresses of five years ago, fashionable restaurants when the vogue has begun to ebb from them.
> (Benjamin 1989: 175)

What the Surrealists managed to do, and what Benjamin himself obviously admired and hoped to imitate was: 'bring the immense forces of "atmosphere" concealed in these things to the point of explosion'. Benjamin wanted to know the answer to the question:

'What form do you suppose a life would take that was determined at a decisive moment precisely by the street song last on
everyone's lips?' (Benjamin 1989: 175)

Despite his own evaluation of the significance of André
Breton, the Surrealist who had the most significant impact on
Benjamin's work and philosophy of history was perhaps Louis
Aragon. In particular, a considerable part of Benjamin's Arcades
work is permeated with the kind of atmosphere contained in
Aragon's book *Paris Peasant* (Aragon 1971). Susan Buck-Morss
notes Benjamin's own statement that when he read Aragon's
book at night in bed, 'I could never read more than two or three
pages before my heartbeat got so strong that I had to put the book
down' (Benjamin quoted in Buck-Morss 1977: 125). The question
is of course precisely why Aragon's book had such a profound
impact on Benjamin. Arguably it was because in *Paris Peasant*
Benjamin found a kindred spirit.

In Aragon's book Benjamin found 'The trick by which this
world of things is mastered – it is more proper to speak of a trick
than of a method' which 'consists in the substitution of a political
for a historical view of the past' (Benjamin 1989: 175). Similarly,
just as Benjamin went to Paris to try to find the hidden secret of
progress, so, for the Surrealists, 'At the centre of this world of
things stands the most dreamed-of of their objects, the city of
Paris itself' (Benjamin 1989: 176). Benjamin sees Paris as a reification in both senses of the word. Firstly, it is a reification because
it is a social and cultural fabrication. Secondly, however, it is a
reification because it is a place which seems to possess its own
natural laws about which humanity can do nothing other than
accommodate itself and revel in the mystery. Benjamin called the
Paris of the Surrealists like Aragon a 'little universe' which is
more or less identical with the cosmos of first nature: 'There too
are crossroads where ghostly signals flash from the traffic, and
inconceivable analogies and connections between events are the
order of the day' (Benjamin 1989: 176–177).

For Aragon, the fabrications which remain without reason
come to possess a mysterious if not positively religious aura.
Progress has led to abandonment and in the abandonment of
obsolescence it is possible to find an alternative to the demand for
perpetual movement forwards. Aragon understands this process
in a dialectical way. On the one hand, progress has tended to
make religion obsolete. Aragon writes that: 'Wandering through

the countryside, I see nothing but abandoned chapels, overturned calvaries. The human pilgrimage has forsaken these stations, for they demanded a far more leisurely pace than the one now adopted' (Aragon 1971: 131). Indeed for Aragon the changing experience of the world has led to changes in the meanings of formerly sacred icons: 'The folds of these Virgins' robes presupposed a process of reflection wholly incompatible with today's principle of acceleration governing movement from one point to another' (Aragon 1971: 131). Yet on the other hand progress has caused the making of new Gods and new desires of heaven: 'Here are great red gods, great yellow gods, great green gods, planted at the edges of the speculative tracks along which the mind speeds from one feeling to another', along which the mind speeds 'from one idea to its consequences in its race for fulfilment' (Aragon 1971: 131).

According to Aragon, technology has become the new God which makes 'destiny and force look so barbaric' (Aragon 1971: 131): 'O Texaco motor oil, Esso, Shell, great inscriptions of human potentiality, soon we shall cross ourselves before your fountains' (Aragon 1971: 132). But these Gods will not last. The objects we presently worship in all their newness and gleaming beauty are themselves fated to obsolescence.

Rather like Benjamin, and certainly in a way which recalls Adorno's critique of Benjamin as a slave to reification, Aragon recorded, 'the great power that certain places, certain sights exercised over me, without discovering the principle of this enchantment. Some everyday objects unquestionably contained for me a part of that mystery, plunged me into that mystery' (Aragon 1971: 128). Aragon sought the secret of that mysterious sense of enchantment and found it in the very anonymity of mundane objects. Aragon discovered that things are materially self-sufficient even as they become socially and culturally meaningless thanks to the onward march of progress: 'The way I saw it, an object became transfigured: it took on neither the allegorical aspect nor the character of the symbol, it did not so much manifest an idea as constitute that very idea.' Indeed, Aragon saw that the object 'extended deeply into the world's mass' (Aragon 1971: 128).

Out of all of this Aragon came to contend that objects provide a way of entering into the recognition of the transitory status of the new. Objective things which are the products of fabrication

turned into reification offer a way of recognizing the history of
the present now; the pastness of the present tense. Aragon looked
at fabrication become reification and 'began to understand that
their kingdom derived its nature from their newness, and that a
mortal star shone over the future of this kingdom. So they
appeared to me in the guise of transitory tyrants' (Aragon 1971:
129). If according to Benjamin this Surrealist methodology is a
trick then it is a trick which Walter Benjamin himself performed
with more than a modicum of expertise. Aragon could well have
been speaking on behalf of Benjamin when he wrote that he, 'set
about discovering the face of the infinite beneath the concrete
forms which were escorting me, walking the length of the earth's
avenues' (Aragon 1971: 130). (This formulation of Aragon's owes
fairly considerable and clear debts to Baudelaire's definition of
modernity.) Similarly, it is almost impossible not to think of
Benjamin's claim that a redemption from history is possible if all
things can be remembered when Aragon is found 'walking tipsily
among countless divine concretions'; divinities which 'live, attain
the zenith of their power, then die, leaving their perfumed altars
to other gods. They are the very principles of every transformation of everything. They are the necessity of movement'
(Aragon 1971: 130).

If it is accepted that Benjamin's 'Theses on the Philosophy of
History' have at least a part of their origins in a sympathetic
encounter with Surrealism and Aragon in particular, then it can
be proposed that what Adorno identifies as the tendency towards
myth in Benjamin can be found to have its roots precisely here.
(With this proposition I am not at all wishing to preclude the
validity of other readings of Benjamin. To recall Rorty's depiction
of inspired reading, the approach I am adopting throughout this
book emphasizes my responses to and readings of texts; the
approach is an attempt to show how I have been forced to change
my interpretations of the world. Nothing I say has the status of
definitive authority.) In so far as Benjamin copied the Surrealists'
trick of profane illumination he was led to create a myth of things
more or less by default. He stumbled into the realm of mystery
which the Surrealists blithely and contentedly wandered into.

Aragon was always quite explicit about his desire to construct
a myth out of the places and objects which he found about him;
the places and objects which had been made anonymous by their
exclusion from progress and the forgetting of their fabrication

(two processes which lead to reification and the experience of the existence of objective things as if by nature). With *Paris Peasant* Aragon wrote a book in the service and illustration of his assertion that: 'New myths spring up beneath each step we take. Legend begins where man has lived, where he lives.... Each day the modern sense of existence becomes subtly altered. A mythology ravels and unravels' (Aragon 1971: 24). But that mythology can only be glimpsed and written up by the person who experiences the world as a series of shocks. The sense of the marvel of the homes humanity has built is impossible for those who, to refer to Benjamin's image, fly on the wings of the Angel of History. According to Aragon, the sense of the marvellous can be seen to 'fade away in every man who advances into his own life as though along an always smoother road, who advances into the world's habits with an increasing ease'. It disappears in those who rid themselves 'progressively of the taste and texture of the unwonted, the unthought of' (Aragon 1971: 24). Benjamin retained a keen sense of the marvellous but he was only able to do that because, as Adorno perhaps rightly complains, Benjamin played on the terrain of the second nature of reification without revealing it for the social and cultural fabrication it truly is. Benjamin thereby did little more than secularize myth.

Benjamin's philosophy of history is a demonstration of the implications and consequences of material and intellectual reification. Benjamin shows what the world might be like, and what might be the chances for a humanization of the human condition, when that world is experienced and apprehended in the finding not the making. Benjamin's methodology (or trick) ultimately relies on a Messianism as the only way of making the case for a redemption which relies on a remembering of the presence of the past and the past of the present. Without that myth, Benjamin would be quite unable to augur the shock of the profane illumination which he so admired when it was produced by the Surrealists, and neither would he be able to indicate, even less occupy the space of the state of emergency.

The analysis of the world which is offered by Walter Benjamin is utterly paradoxical. It demonstrates nothing other than the deep hold and powerful sway of all of the arrangements and relationships which Benjamin actually desired to try to overcome. What Benjamin seems to indicate is that only a few options remain to those who are the children of the fabricators of the things which distinguish the objectivity of the human condition as opposed to the dull processes of animal life. Benjamin seems to indicate that as the second meaning of reification comes to dominate over the first the opportunities for social and cultural action are more and more hemmed in by restraints which are experienced as allowing for no dispute.

In so far as the dialectic of reification remains unbroken, only three kinds of experiences of the world seem to be possible to imagine. The first experience is one of a reverie in the fabricated human house which now becomes a house of the dead populated with the poltergeists of myth, Messianism and a mundane mystery. The second experience is one of an ironic re-establishment of the myth of progress; certainly the Angel of History might see a pile of debris and certainly the Angel might be caught in a hurricane, but he is still going somewhere and perhaps he can take us too. We might not know where we are going but perhaps anywhere is better than this haunted and ghostly time and place. The third experience is one not of the response of shock to the realization of the presence of the past and the past of the present but, instead, the response of relief and a sense of safety. An idea of this kind of response is stimulated by Georges Bataille.

Bataille once wrote about what he took to be common emotions when one gazes upon photographs of one's ancestors. According to Bataille: 'The mere sight (in photography) of our predecessors . . . now produces . . . a burst of loud and raucous laughter; that sight, however, is nonetheless hideous' (Bataille 1986: 17). The laughter and the horror are due to the 'tiresome absurdity' of our ancestors who photography reveal to be too small and too much like us to have been able to have carried out the great deeds attributed to them by the myth of progress. The responses are also due to the ability of photographs from the past to conjure up 'those vain ghosts' of whom 'we seem to have spent the greater part of our time in obliterating all traces, even the smallest, of that shameful ancestry' (Bataille 1986: 17).

Taken at face value, Bataille's comments lend to photographs precisely that ability to produce the shock of crystallization and the state of emergency which Benjamin lends to his method-ology-trick of history. But what Bataille provides is a somewhat partial depiction of responses at seeing photographs of ancestors. It is certainly the case that we frequently laugh at such images.

Quite often they are indeed ludicrous because of changes of fashion. Photographs can also produce a shock because of our inability to work out exactly why this picture of this someone no one remembers is in our collection. Following Bataille, those kinds of question marks might well inspire a laughter which is in part a laughter of absurdity mingled with horror. But it is also a laughter of relief. It is a relief at how far we have come in such a short period of time (so that for the eternal present moment of the looking at the images we do not wear unfashionable clothes, we do not have hair which is either too long or too short); relief that despite the mysteries of faces from the past we know exactly who we are and who the others are who look at our family albums (we share the mystery of not knowing the name of the soldier from 1916 and so we are brought together; for us the photograph becomes mythic if not indeed an icon which helps us make sense of who we are, where we have come from and where we are going).

The conclusion seems to be clear. The dialectic of reification has reduced the opportunities and horizons of humanity to sight-seeing in the museum of the house of the dead. Benjamin and Surrealism alike offer the chance of adventures, but those adventures necessarily have to leave the museum and the things it contains more or less wholly unchallenged. Reification is thus the precondition for what we are and what we might aspire to be. Neither Benjamin nor Surrealism offers any critique or challenge to the tendency of fabrications to become like a second nature. Instead they write an ecstatic celebration of it.

The dialectic of reification implies a process in which social and cultural construction becomes 'museal'. This word comes from Adorno and he says that: 'It describes objects to which the observer no longer has a vital relationship and which are in the process of dying.' Adorno continues to suggest that these objects: 'owe their preservation more to historical respect than to the needs of the present' (Adorno 1967: 175). These objects have their homes in the museums which are 'like the family sepulchres of works of art. They testify to the naturalization of culture' (Adorno 1967: 175). The naturalization of culture means that human fabrications cease to be experienced as social and cultural constructions and as the products of work. Similarly, they cease to be experienced as vital at any level greater than the ability attributed to them to lend a gloss of timelessness and traditional authenticity to what happens to take place and exist here and now. In these ways, and as Benjamin and the Surrealists make abundantly clear, the museal situation is one in which the objective attitude which identifies nature as a mute thing out there waiting to have violence practised upon it ceases to be tenable. The dividing line between the human and the natural becomes too blurred for it to allow for that kind of certainty and, indeed, for it to allow for any confidence that violence is aimed in the appropriate direction.

If fabrication requires an experience of nature which is essentially contained within and described by Weber's concept of disenchantment, then fabrication which is imprisoned (as it necessarily is imprisoned) within the dialectic of reification actually evinces a tendency towards the enchantment of second nature. Social and cultural constructions come to possess a magical and mystical quality which is experienced as being all their own and quite beyond the ambitions and intent of their human fabricators. For Benjamin, the magic and mystery resides in the ability of things to imply a recollection, remembering and monadic crystallization of all pasts and all presents into a state of emergency in which it is possible to prepare for the moment of redemption. For Aragon that magical quality distils into a fairly hallucinatory world in which mundane commonplaces can be shocked into something different through the ability of things to stand outside and beyond the time of history, the time in which the past has disappeared because of the arrival of today.

The human ability to make the human world has been dramatically reduced. Benjamin and the Surrealists write about a human condition which is imagined as only liable to fabrication to the extent that certain pre-existing raw materials can be assumed to be available to be found. As reification becomes second nature the core of the human condition is reworked; not making but finding, not mute and passive nature but enchanted second nature. And that, in turn, means that it becomes very difficult to know what humanity itself might involve.

3

CONSUMING

With his metaphor of the disenchantment of the world Max Weber expressed one of the central myths by which fabrication is understood and intellectually spurred on to ever greater feats of construction. Indeed, perhaps Weber's image (which, it ought to be said, owes far more to a literary than to a specifically socio-logical imagination), has proved to be so popular and compelling precisely because it resonates so well with the practical belief that the human condition necessarily involves the social and cultural fabrication of homes fit for men and women to live in for all time. Take away the sense of melancholy which pervades what Weber says about disenchantment and what remains is, essentially, a myth of fabrication which tells a story of ever greater objectivity and ever greater humanity and humanization. (Although for Weber of course that humanization is a rather poisoned chalice; without the get-out clause of the charismatic leader it implies nothing other than the opening up of the iron cage of bureaucracy. As such, Weber tells a normative tale which fits in with the narrative structure of rise, decline and fall; from enchantment to disenchantment to rationality.)

At the heart of Weber's metaphor is the contention that disen-chantment may be understood as a process which is set in train by empirical knowledge: 'empirical knowledge has consistently worked through to the disenchantment of the world and its trans-formation into a causal mechanism' (Weber 1948: 350). In other words, disenchantment is about the identification of an objective world out there which stands in mute opposition to the subjective world in here. That out there is commonly called nature and it is understood to obey processual laws which are taken to exist like mechanisms and can only be known from the point of view of socially and culturally generated empirical knowledge. The out there has no subjective animating principle of its own since subjectivity is a purely social and cultural possession and condition. In its own terms, disenchantment demonstrates that the universe has no non-mechanistic definite meaning except for the kind of meaning which is predicated upon a leap of faith and which is, therefore, pushed beyond self-awareness and the possibility of empirical knowing (in other words, empirical knowledge allows for a ghost in the machine only to the extent that the ghost can never get in the way of empirically based activity. The ghost is allowed to exist only so long as it does not actually make too much of a difference to anything other than the quest of individuals to make life make sense).

Weber makes it clear that disenchantment consists in the bringing to bear of a corrosive, relentless, glare of suspicion on all claims to meaningfulness: 'In principle, the empirical as well as the mathematically oriented view of the world develops refutations of every intellectual approach which in any way asks for a "meaning" of inner-worldly occurrences' (Weber 1948: 351). In this light it might well be said that disenchantment implies the subjection of humanity and human being to the Archimedean point which was, Hannah Arendt emphasizes, one of the devices by and through which humanity was separated out from the rest of the surrounding world. Consequently, humanity is turned into a thoroughly ambivalent figure. On the one hand it is something to be known as an out there, just like nature, but on the other hand humanity is the subject and the agent of that knowing; humanity is also in here. (This kind of ambivalence is emphasized by Michel Foucault in *The Order of Things*; see Foucault 1970. Kurt Wolff draws on a hermeneutic tradition to register a somewhat similar account of the status of human being when he distinguishes between human being as subject who searches for meaning and human being as object which is the site and occasion of meaning; see Wolff 1989. Once again there is the suspicion that a lot of what Foucault said was already common currency for some others.)

According to Weber the process of disenchantment was originally a Western phenomenon (and in his important Introduction to *The Protestant Ethic and the Spirit of Capitalism*, Weber makes it plain that his own work has its roots and trajectory in the process of disenchantment. More generally it can therefore be asserted that sociology is at least in part a study in the service of disenchantment – but this identification of the basis of sociology also means that the discipline can therefore be an agent of the iron cage; see Weber 1930: 13–31. But sociology is also a potential servant of re-enchantment to the extent that it naturalizes intellectual constructions and imaginations. It is that dialectic of disenchantment and re-enchantment which runs through the moral problem of what it means to do sociology, what it means to be a sociologist.)

Weber claims that it is in 'the Occident' that the process of disenchantment remains most pronounced (Weber 1948: 139). It is this belief which is one explanation of the methodological conundrum which Weber poses at the beginning of *The Protestant Ethic* of precisely how it has been that social and cultural artifacts could have moved beyond the West and into evidently universal significance (Weber 1930: 13). He understands disenchantment as the principle that: 'there are no mysterious incalculable forces that come into play, but rather that one can . . . master all things by calculation'. Consequently: 'One need no longer have recourse to magical means in order to master or implore the spirits, as did the savage, for whom such mysterious powers existed. Technical means and calculations perform the service' (Weber 1948: 139).

For Weber then, disenchantment is a process grounded in an attitude towards the world which has practical implications in so far as it banishes the fear that spirits might lurk in things. It thus inspires an objectivity which treats the world of things experienced as out there as a resource waiting to be used. This is a metaphor which is highly abstract but all the more seductive for that. The story Weber tells can carry on regardless of local difficulties. Disenchantment becomes a general process which can be taken to be more true than the thereby contingent circumstances which individuals face in their day-to-day lives and relationships.

Weber was subtle enough to know that disenchantment might be a somewhat more ambivalent process than the main story and dominant principles within the metaphor would seem to allow. Weber was at least implicitly aware of the possibility that disenchantment might itself imply a consolidation of the spell of enchantment even as the base of that enchantment is increasingly narrowed. Weber argued that even as disenchantment makes religious beliefs seem to be little more than superstition, it is nevertheless the case that such beliefs and such experiences of the world might become ever more untouchable by disenchantment itself. They increasingly operate on a wholly different terrain than empirical investigation and thus come to be somewhat immune or incidental to it. As Weber puts the matter: 'Every increase of rationalism in empirical science increasingly pushes religion from the rational into the irrational realm; but only today does religion become the irrational or anti-rational supra-human power' (Weber 1948: 351). Attitudes based in faith (that is, religious attitudes towards and understandings of the world) thus retain a legitimacy and authority precisely to the extent that they are exempted from any kind of rational proof or even, perhaps, pragmatic usefulness. This is what their evident irrationality comprises. They command allegiance despite the rational world revealed through empirical knowledge and not at all because of it.

When he claims that science makes religion increasingly irrational but therefore ever more powerfully supra-human, Weber is implicitly recognizing two things. Firstly, he is recognizing the possibility that disenchantment is not such a simple and straightforward process as its confident and strident narrative might claim. Weber is aware that the process can be assumed to generate resistance and opposition. Weber actually knows that despite its insight and usefulness, the metaphor of disenchantment tends to oversimplify complex social and cultural relationships (and implicitly he might therefore also be aware of the likelihood that there is more to social and cultural arrangements and relationships than sociological narratives might be able to say). Secondly, Weber is recognizing the formal point that disenchantment and enchantment are not pure situations which exist in complete isolation from one another. Weber is recognizing that they are situations which exist in a relationship of dialectical tension. The one requires and produces the other. After all, without its other of enchantment there would be little purpose to disenchantment since nothing and nowhere would be able to be identified as enchanted in the first place. The negation produces that which it is invested with the role and the purpose of negating.

The unfortunate thing is how Weber so quickly and unproblematically reduces the powers and the milieu of enchantment to religion. Admittedly, the term religion might be used to refer to any and all series of beliefs which assume the legitimacy of something beyond the empirical and the rational knowing, but Weber seems to operate with a somewhat more restricted definition than that. Certainly, experiences of the world which emphasize a high level of belief in enchantment might well be cast of a frequently religious mould, but that is not to say that all experiences and apprehensions of enchantment are therefore identical with religion as such. Enchantment is not just religious, and it is certainly not identical with religion to the exclusion of all else. Enchantment is a quality which social and cultural fabrications might also come to possess. More concisely yet; it might be said that Weber misses the distinct possibility that the social and cultural process of disenchantment might itself be liable to tendencies towards enchantment (a tendency which Weber's own work could be identified as contributing towards since it can be taken to paint a future of omniscient rationality or heroic leaders who come as if from nowhere).

At a general conceptual level, this possibility of the tendency towards the enchantment of the social and cultural has two dominant aspects. Firstly, it is possible that the process of disenchantment might itself come to be experienced as if it exists by nature (as if it is actually a construction and not at all a deconstruction of natural artifice). Weber makes it plain that, because of some series of relationships he cannot really explain, disenchantment is a process which comes to seem to be quite universal through its movement beyond its home in 'the Occident'. And as Aristotle argued and Agnes Heller maintains, that which is evidently universal to all social and cultural relationships is likely to be experienced as natural and necessary to such relationships. Secondly, although the process of disenchantment might involve the revelation of the conceit, contingencies and plain stupidities of every existing practice and idea, it can never turn its Archimedean gaze upon itself. For disenchantment to be able to proceed apace, the validity of disenchantment can never be opened up to scrutiny. If the authority of the case for disenchantment is investigated it becomes perfectly clear that there is no necessary reason or justification for it other than the utterly irrational assertion that disenchantment simply must take place. The meaning and authority of disenchantment can never itself be known for the simple reason that there is nothing to be known. Without its blind assertion and dull acceptance disenchantment has no authority whatsoever. It merely seems to be grounded in some authority and legitimacy because it successfully demolishes any

competing perspectives and claims. In these terms, disenchantment might be defined as a Socratic procedure; all it does is
question other principles and procedures without ever saying
what it involves itself.

It is then distinctly possible that disenchantment is itself liable
to become experienced as a form of enchantment. That enchantment consists in the tendencies for disenchantment seemingly to
come to exist as if by nature and for its authority evidently to be
grounded in some place which is outside and beyond the orbit of
social and cultural critical self-awareness (ultimately, disenchantment rests its case on what amounts to a leap of faith which
asserts that it is a good or a necessary process). It can be proposed
that disenchantment implies a process which contains a tendency
towards the partial re-enchantment of the world. This tendency
becomes explicit in so far as there arises a sense and an experience
of the possibility that some crucial aspect of the world always
exists beyond human designs, ambitions and understandings.
That 'something beyond' is the very authority of and for the
disenchantment which is meant to demonstrate that actually there
is no 'beyond'.

But the tendency towards re-enchantment which goes hand in
hand with the process of disenchantment operates at a far more
ordinary level than all of this. As Walter Benjamin and the
Surrealists realized, re-enchantment is a quality which tends to
surround commodities. Commodities are social and cultural productions which, in capitalist relationships, take on the air of
existing quite independently of any activities of the production.
(For my own part I would want to speculate that this transformation in the experiential status of commodities is not peculiar to
capitalism alone; it probably also occurred in the situations of
long ago which were once known as Really Existing Socialism. I
would want to speculate that all commodities are liable to
become surrounded with an air of independence because of their
potential existence on a spatial and temporal terrain which is not
necessarily identical to or even compatible with the spatial and
temporal awareness of individuals or social and cultural groups.)

As such, commodities can be identified as a very precise, important and ordinary instance of the processes which I have been
understanding in terms of what I am calling the dialectic of
reification. On the one hand commodities are reified in so far as
they are social and cultural fabrications (this aspect of the dialectic

56

might usefully be labelled Reification I; it relates to the meaning of reification which Hannah Arendt stresses). Yet on the other hand commodities are things which tend to be apprehended as existing on their own, on a basis of self-sufficiency; they tend to come to stand apart from and over and above the circumstances of their fabrication (this aspect of the dialectic might usefully be labelled Reification II; it relates to the meaning of reification which Hannah Arendt underemphasizes). To put exactly the same point into somewhat different terminology, it can be proposed that commodities stand as one of the clearest possible examples of the dialectical process whereby things which are made tend to be experienced and confronted as things which can only be found.

All of this has been known since Karl Marx developed his account of commodity fetishism in the first volume of *Capital*. There, Marx attempted to explain why and how commodities are the subjects of an exchange value which is more than their pure use value or cost of production. Marx wanted to know why consumers find commodities so very alluring. He wanted to know why we tend to invest commodities with much greater value than their simple use would imply. When a commodity is analysed purely in terms of its use value there is actually very little to be said about it. Whether it is explored in terms of the ability of its properties to satisfy wants or 'from the point that those properties are the product of human labour', 'It is as clear as noon-day, that man, by his industry, changes the forms of the materials furnished by nature, in such a way as to make them useful to him' (Marx 1938: 41). (This point is more or less identical in its thrust if not its terminology with Arendt's emphasis on the violence towards nature which fabrication involves.) But Marx knew that this was not the whole story. The commodity must be about something rather more than simple use value if it is to possess an exchange value which will generate profit. It has to be turned into something which is wanted and desired rather than just needed (and an indication that this transformation does indeed occur is the simple fact that we frequently want things which we do not need in order to satisfy the demands of material life). As such: 'the table continues to be that common, every-day thing, wood. But, so soon as it steps forth as a commodity it is changed into something transcendent' (Marx 1938: 41–42).

It is this aura of transcendence that is the basis of the situation in which human labour is reduced to the exchange value of things and 'the mutual relations of the producers, within which the social character of their labour affirms itself, takes the form of a social relation between the products' (Marx 1938: 42). Here then, Reification I (fabrication) takes the social and cultural form of Reification II (independent standing apart): 'it is a definite social relation between men, that assumes, in their eyes, the fantastic form of a relation between things' (Marx 1938: 43). (Compare with Lukács on second nature and reification.) Commodity fetishism consists in the situation in which: 'A commodity is therefore a mysterious thing, simply because in it the social character of men's labour appears to them as an objective character stamped upon the product of that labour' (Marx 1938: 43). (This statement obviously continues themes in Marx's account of alienation in the *Manuscripts of 1844* (1977).) The world of commodities become free- standing things is comparable only to the world of religion: 'In that world the productions of the human brain appear as independent beings endowed with life, entering into relation both with one another and the human race.' Marx goes on to explain: 'So it is in the world of commodities with the products of men's hands. This I call the Fetishism which attaches itself to the products of labour, so soon as they are produced as commodities' (Marx 1938: 43).

These insights have been developed and illustrated by Wolfgang Fritz Haug in his important work on commodity aesthetics. Haug at once provides a philosophical development of the kinds of points which Marx made, yet he also attempts to use that body of theory to pin down and explain processes and relationships surrounding commodities in mundane everyday life. To this extent then it is clear that Haug owes debts not just to Marx but also to Walter Benjamin. Haug defines precisely what the term commodity aesthetics means: 'It designates a complex which springs from the commodity form of the products and which is functionally determined by exchange value.' As such, commodity aesthetics refers to: 'a complex of material phenomena and of the sensual subject–object relations conditioned by these phenomena' (Haug 1986: 7). In other words, Haug is concerned with the qualities which surround objects and which lend those objects an exchange value which is greater than their use or production value.

Haug derives his understanding of the commodity from Marx but adds to its analysis the original dimension of aesthetics (although of course a discussion of aesthetics is one of the unexplored by-ways in Marx's own discussion of commodity fetishism). For Haug, the term aesthetics has two main meanings in so far as it is coupled with the commodity form. Firstly, aesthetics means 'an appearance which appeals to the senses'. Secondly, aesthetics means 'a beauty developed in the service of the realization of exchange value, whereby commodities are designed to stimulate in the onlooker the desire to possess and the impulse to buy' (Haug 1986: 8). Consequently, Haug pays particular attention to the relationship between commodity aesthetics and the responses which the implications of beauty elicit from the actual or potential consumer.

Haug puts experience at the very centre of the kinds of problems which arise in the tensions of what I have chosen to call the dialectic of reification. Because he understands commodities in terms of their appearances or implications of beauty (that is, because he understands commodities aesthetically and primarily in terms of their image), Haug stresses 'the fascination of aesthetic images'. He continues to clarify what such fascination implies for the experience of commodities: 'Fascination means simply that these aesthetic images capture people's sensuality. In the course of dominating one's sensuality, the fascinated individual is dominated by his or her own senses' (Haug 1986: 45). The image of beauty takes such a deep grip that we simply must have the commodity; we are dominated by our desire which the image of beauty stimulates.

According to Haug, commodity aesthetics mean that the lure of the image can be projected into households as a kind of vanguard for the commodity itself. The image comes in through such means as advertising and serves to create the desires which only the specific object can possibly assuage. The beautiful image, 'becomes completely disembodied and drifts unencumbered like a multicoloured spirit of the commodity into every household, preparing the way for the real distribution of the commodity' (Haug 1986: 50). Image first, sensual need first; commodity second, satisfaction second. As Haug continues to say of the appeal of the image: 'No one is safe any longer from its amorous glances, which the realization motive casts at the consumers with the detached yet technically perfect appearance of a highly promising use value' (Haug 1986: 50). The image and the exchange value first; the use value second.

Precisely because of this situation in which commodity aesthetics creates the desires only the commodity can satisfy, capitalism is able to go on reproducing itself, and the hold of the images of beauty becomes increasingly tenacious (indeed, and going a little beyond Haug's own book, it is quite clear from the logic of his argument that the aesthetic images of commodities can become independent to such an extent that the actual appearance of the commodity is little more than a pleasant surprise): 'An innumerable series of images are forced upon the individual . . . which bring their secrets to the surface and display them there. In these images, people are continually shown the unfulfilled aspects of their existence.' Consequently: 'The illusion ingratiates itself, promising satisfaction: it reads desires in one's eyes, and brings them to the surface of the commodity' (Haug 1986: 52).

Haug's work represents an important contribution to any understanding of exactly how it can be that social and cultural productions seem to exist independently of any relationships and practices of their production. Working beyond the terrain of Haug's own analysis, it can be argued that the point is, of course, that the kind of beauty which commodity aesthetics generates and implies is something which is completely detached from the individual who has been stimulated into needing the commodity. As the old adage says, beauty is in the eye of the beholder. But it only gets into the eye because the beautiful thing is experienced and apprehended as always already existing out there. Beauty is a quality derived from a detached and distanced contemplation; it is not a quality which is known and discovered through action. Beauty is a quality which is found not made. And so the beautiful thing also is experi- entially found not made.

It would be quite wrong to underestimate the importance of media advertising in this process by which the image precedes the commodity. It is thanks to the almost symbiotic relationship between the media and advertising that this process is able to occur. But there is something more to the aura of enchantment which surrounds commodities. After all, advertising makes such great claims for the commodity that if it appears at all then it has to at least look as if it is going to satisfy all of the desires the image has created. It is one thing to make individuals go to a shop to seek out a commodity, but then they have to be persuaded to actually buy it. (Although of course for the advertising agencies the equation is slightly different. The agencies are relatively unconcerned about whether the commodity is actually purchased. They are more concerned about whether they can sell themselves to the provider of the commodity. Advertising is also about the aesthetic creation of the desires which only the advertising agencies can solve. Perhaps in the last instance advertising is about the stimulation of the desire to consume advertising.) The relationships Haug discusses and explores only work to the extent that they do not just make me want a commodity; I also have to be made to feel compelled to part with money in order to possess it. Commodity aesthetics is not a benevolent movement.

The qualities which represent something like the 'value added' to the relationships and insinuations of commodity aesthetics are derived from the spatial situations of the purchasing of commodities. It can be proposed that commodities are attractive not just because of whatever qualities and promises they might seem to possess or make in themselves but also, and this to a very important extent, because of the spaces and places in which commodities are found prior to the moment of their being purchased. As Rob Shields notes: 'Every epoch has its cathedrals, monuments to the era, that come to signify or embody the cultural *Weltanschauung*' (Shields 1992: 3). In the situation of things become images (of fabrications tending to become enchanted; of Reification I tending to shift into Reification II), those cathedrals are the shopping malls.

Shopping malls are the cathedrals of commodity aesthetics because they are places which attract individuals by their promise of satisfaction. Shopping malls overwhelm the visitors with their sheer size, self-sufficiency and removal from the hurly-burly of the outside world. Like cathedrals, shopping malls are experienced as places of escape from routine and as opportunities for adventures in pilgrimage (in so far as a pilgrimage is a journey in search of something which will make the journey worthwhile). Irrespective of how noisy they might actually be, shopping malls invariably seem to be very quiet and even quite peaceful. Shopping malls are entries into a world apart; into a different sort of world which compensates for the struggles and tribulations experienced in getting there. The shopping mall is the world as it could be which thus tempers the appeal and attraction of the world as it is: 'In the malls . . . everything is larger, the architecture more monumental.' Everything is here, waiting to be used: 'the major "anchor stores" multiply and the functions increase with the addition of cinemas, hotels, zoos, recreation complexes featuring pools, ice-rinks, stadia, fairground rides and so on' (Shields 1992: 4).

Shopping malls are worth a degree of consideration because they stand in a line of succession with the Arcades of Paris which were emphasized so much by Walter Benjamin and Louis Aragon. Like the Arcades, the shopping malls can be identified as an expression of a present 'now' which will, thanks to the terrible flight of the Angel of History, come to be consigned to a present moment from and of the past. The lesson of the Arcades is that the shopping malls which are so dazzling and brilliant today will eventually come to be apprehended and experienced as little more than flawed attempts to attain the shopping complexes of the future. (To this extent it is only necessary to think of the fate of the shopping centres of the 1960s and 1970s; when they were built they were as wonderful and contemporary as the shopping malls are to us. Now they are either dead spaces in town centres, pale copies of what came to pass, or artifacts in the history of neo-brutalist architecture built on the cheap.) Benjamin shows that the shopping malls of this present moment will become like the pottery shards of archaeologists; they will be remnants which will need to be put together by the archaeologists of future presents who will wish to see how their forebears existed. Meanwhile Aragon shows that the shopping malls will tend to become increasingly surreal as they become increasingly obsolete. However, if this combination of magic and mystery is likely to be the future of the shopping paradises of this present moment, it is not to say that they do not possess a degree of wonder here and now. (Of course, none of this is to offer any picture whatsoever of what the future might be like; all I am speculating about is what the present might come to look like if Benjamin and Aragon are used to understand the nature of history. For sociology the future is, and ought always to remain, a completely closed book. It is only in that way that the future can remain open.)

The shopping mall is indeed a magical place in and for the present moment. It is a site of enchantment. Firstly, it is magical because it is dedicated to one kind of activity which is consequently elevated to the status of being the secret of existence in this specific time and place. It is magical because it is the site and the place of a complete universe which provides answers to all the questions which are addressed to it. (It can certainly offer the answers to the old philosophical problems: where am I? why am I? what am I?) Quite without empirical reason, the shopping mall establishes one truth as the truth (the truth of shopping; the truth which is established on the basis of a leap of faith on the ground of the desires stimulated by commodity aesthetics). It provides the means by which that truth can be practised (in shops with aesthetically beautiful commodities). Secondly, the mall is magical because the objects it contains betray no trace of the processes and relationships of their fabrication. Instead they exist solely in terms of the relationships of exchange and the commitments of credit required by and for their consumption. (As such the promise of pleasure and happiness which the aesthetic image has stimulated can be satisfied through certain kinds of ascetic practices. Perhaps the worshippers in these cathedrals make their confessions to the credit agency.) Thirdly, the shopping mall is seemingly magical because it is likely that there will be little or no memory of the time before its existence; it will in fact be apprehended as like a second nature. It is important to note that in Britain at least, shopping malls are invariably built on sites which were previously wasteland or first nature.

But it would be quite wrong to identify a common experience in relation to these palaces of enchantment. Not all social and cultural groups have the same experiences in relation to the shopping malls and the illusions-become-objects which they contain. It might seem like a crassly and simplistically Marxist thing to say, but the shopping malls can only be experienced as opportunities for the satisfaction of desires by individuals who have to hand the material means by which they might be able to purchase things. Even though everyone might be urged to buy into the beautiful world conjured up by commodity aesthetics, it is nevertheless the case that only some individuals can buy the commodities which promise to satisfy all their deepest needs and desires. There is a world of difference between standing in the window shopping and window-shopping.

In other words, the dialectic of reification is not an analytic affair alone. It can also be seen to be playing itself out in everyday social and cultural relationships. Some social and cultural groups and individuals can purchase the pleasures of the magical mysteries of Reification II, and can pretend that those things exist as if by nature because those very things are fabricated by other social and cultural groups which are either ignored, forgotten or hidden away. Our magic is the product of their labour; our enchantments are purchased on the back of their imprisonment in the iron cage of rationality which emerges in the wake of disenchantment. The situation of consumption, the situation of the enjoyment of the pleasures and the satisfaction of the desires of Reification II, is predicated on the activity of others who are likely to be ignored or simply not noticed and who are, by virtue of our very pleasures and desires, consigned to the fabrication which is the defining activity of the condition of Reification I.

In Arendt's terms, consignment to fabrication might not be an entirely bad thing. Indeed, in her terms it could even be argued that the occupants of the situations of Reification I lead an extremely honest existence which is framed by the integrity and the responsibilities of the fabrication of the objects which will demarcate and establish the homes for humanity in the world. They know the dignity of labour. In ontological and philosophical terms that is as may be. But the problem is that social and cultural groups do not necessarily fit in too neatly with ontological and philosophical arguments. The point is that the fabricators of Reification I are not free labourers (a point which Marx demonstrated in one way and Weber demonstrated in another way with his analysis of the compulsions of the Protestant ethic), and neither are they ignorant of the desires stimulated by commodity aesthetics. They want the commodities too; they want to purchase this little bit (or is it a large bit?) of happiness. But they cannot.

Quite simply, an object in a shop is hardly likely to be magical for me if I participated in the making of it. I will know in advance that there is a disjuncture between the aesthetic bliss of the image and the ordinary existence of the commodity (a disjuncture every child knows when it receives the toy it saw advertised on the television; the real thing is always extremely disappointing; a disjuncture every man knows when he discovers that his smooth-shave and aftershave does not cause others to swoon at his feet. But of course the disjuncture just leads to the reproduction of commodity aesthetics. The disappointment is not the razor blade's; the disappointment is due to my having cut myself). Indeed I am very likely to react to the presence of the thing I made by declaring that 'I would never buy one of those – I know how it is put together'.

But of course the division of labour means that not too many individuals are likely to have that kind of direct one-on-one relationship with the commodity since they will not have made it as such. At most, all the individual is likely to have made is one component. But then again, in so far as an increasingly dominant proportion of the working population is not employed in any kind of manufacturing activity, then the commodity will be approached as a pre-existing independent thing which is just there. Here then the division of labour might well be identified as a contributing cause towards the enchantment of the world in so far as it means that more and more people experience the world in its finding and not its making. (I am very aware of the Eurocentrism of that paragraph; the division of labour is of course now written on a global canvas. Here I am writing about relationships and experiences as they might be defining of the situations of individuals; and individuals are rarely too concerned about what happens beyond the confines of their own little worlds of meaning and meaningfulness. Moreover I am not at all sure that the kind of sociology I carry out can be extended beyond Europe and its inventions in Australasia and America.)

As if to symbolize this dialectic wherein some social and cultural groups are able to live the dreams of the enchanted situation of commodity aesthetics only because other groups are out of sight and out of mind making the commodities (a dialectical situation which of course relates to conventional class analysis but is in fact much broader than that), it is only necessary to think of the design of shopping malls. It is tempting to speculate that the design of shopping malls can be read as a metaphor for the social and cultural relationships thrown up by the dialectic of reification. Like the dialectic itself, the design of the shopping mall indicates a situation in which any talk or conceit of a universal human condition is, from a sociological point of view, little more than wishful thinking.

Certainly, everyone inside the shopping mall can enjoy the pleasures of commodity aesthetics, but one of the hardest things to do with a shopping mall is find the way in. Moreover, anybody who walks to the mall is confronted with the danger of getting run over by a car which will deliver its passengers to the shops before the walker will ever arrive. Consequently, it is quite wrong, cretinous and stupid to suppose that commodity aesthetics and shopping malls mean the same to everyone. They do not. Money and separation from fabrication is needed if the individual is going to be able to satisfy her or his desires. And those without money have to be forced or persuaded to accept their perpetual dissatisfaction.

Zygmunt Bauman has offered the metaphor of Thélèmic society to understand precisely these kinds of relationships. (I want to take up Bauman's metaphor for my own purposes. He develops it in terms of an analysis of social and cultural relationships which is a little different to the analysis I am seeking to develop here: Bauman 1988.) The image of Thélème is taken from Rabelais's *Gargantua*. According to Bauman: 'Thélème is the place of gracious living; wealth is here the moral virtue, happiness the main commandment, pleasure the purpose of life, taste the major skill, amusement the paramount art, enjoyment the only duty' (Bauman 1988: 92). In other words, Thélème is a place of enchantment. Bauman continues to point out that all of this pleasure requires certain means of defence and protection if it is going to be possible on a relatively long-term basis: 'The most remarkable feature of Thélème is its thick walls. Inside, one has no occasion to worry where the wealth, the happiness and amusements come from' (Bauman 1988: 92). The walls of Thélème are then a symbol of the line of division between two different social and cultural groups which can be understood as existing in different situations in relation to the dialectic of reification; between those who can buy or find their way into the pleasure palace and those others who are kept outside (or who are only allowed in as servants or as sites of gratification for the insiders). I will call the insiders the consumers and I will call the outsiders the fabricators.

The thick wall is a crucial part of the architecture of this Thélèmic situation. It does more than simply demarcate the boundary line between the in and the out groups (between the consumers and the fabricators respectively). The wall means that the consumers on the inside never have to confront the costs and the circumstances of the fabrication of what it is that they enjoy: 'the sweatshops, the non-unionized and helpless labour, the misery of living on the dole, of having the wrong skin colour, the agony of being unneeded and wished out of existence' (Bauman 1988: 92). The thick wall means that the consumers never have to think about all of these pressing issues which are thrown up by the procedures, the relationships and the lived experiences of fabrication (indeed, for the consumers these precisely are not pressing issues).

It is helpful to use this image to try to understand the social and cultural implications of the different subject positions contained within, and created by, the dialectic of reification. The consumers are removed from the compunctions of Reification I (from the compunctions of fabrication and what for them becomes defined as the dirty business of doing violence to material nature). They play entirely on the terrain of the socially and culturally constructed second nature and have no relationships whatsoever with first nature except in so far as it has been turned into the surroundings of leisure amenities (by way of an illustrative anecdote: in the area where I live, first nature is little more than the woody bit between golf courses). Thanks to their access to financial resources and their isolation from relationships of manufacturing production (from fabrication itself), these social and cultural groups are consumers of things produced by others who are invisible or forgotten. These groups have the ability to buy themselves out of the work of the making of the objects which underpin the human condition. Either that or they are quite divorced from fabrication because of their position in the division of labour.

The groups which are defined by and structured around the relationships and experiences of fabrication (who are, as it were, somewhat unable to find their way into the enchantment of the shopping malls) have a rather contrary situation. Precisely because of their lack of access to secure financial resources and precisely because of their (however partial and however tenuous) involvement in the activity of fabrication, they are unable to participate with ease in the pleasures of consuming even though commodity aesthetics make them feel a need so to do. They are too busy labouring and working for that.

Consequently, it is not too useful to follow what has become tradition and suggest that any social and cultural relationships which emphasize consumption can thereby be defined globally as a consumer society. There are at least two very major shortcomings with the concept of consumer society. Firstly, it establishes a single activity as the defining trait of all social and cultural relationships (it is then actually something by way of a product of enchantment). But consumption cannot possibly be any single or universal truth for the rather simple reason that

there can only be consumption if there has already been fabrication. We do not consume ideas or mental abstractions alone
(although commodity aesthetics demonstrates that we do consume abstractions for at least some of the time). We consume
objective things which have to be fabricated somewhere by
someone. To this extent then the concept of consumer society
precludes any discussion whatsoever of what it is that is
consumed. The concept of consumer society means that we, to
paraphrase William Burroughs, will be unable to see what is on
the end of our fork (and, of course, how it got there). Secondly,
the concept is problematic because it clings to a notion of a
unitary and a single 'society'. But if it is legitimate to suggest that
the articulations of the human condition have been pluralized
along the line of division between the activities and the practices
of fabrication and consumption then it is hard to see how it can be
supposed that there is any single thing called society. It would
seem to make more sense to talk in terms of different situations of
social and cultural arrangements, institutions and relationships
and to analyse the complex encounters between them rather than
to suggest that they all come together into a single entity which in
some way tends to hold together in the end.

If this series of speculations is reasonable then it has a number
of very serious implications. It means that Arendt's account of the
human condition will have to be rewritten so that it can contain a
fourth principle of articulation; the principle of consumption
would have to be added to those of labour, work and action.
Consumption can be defined as the use of the fabrications of
work. The human condition of consumption will thereby be
commodity aesthetics. Moreover, it will not be too helpful to
understand consumption as a false or artificial kind of freedom;
it will have to be understood as a dimension or possibility of
human being in the world which has its own freedoms and its
own virtues.

This is a much stronger understanding of consumption than
Arendt allows. Certainly Arendt is aware of the activity of consumption but she is only prepared to identify it as an aspect of
labour. For Arendt: 'labor and consumption are but two stages of
the same process, imposed upon man by the necessity of life'.
According to Arendt to say that we live in a consumers' society
'is only another way of saying that we live in a society of laborers'
(Arendt 1958: 110). However, Arendt's point only holds good on

the basis of the assumption of a single and universal human condition (also it only holds good if we forget about the ability of commodity aesthetics to make us want things we do not need to secure the means of material life). In Arendt's terms it is indeed quite reasonable to identify a line of continuity between labour and consumption. But if there is a split between fabrication and consumption then labour and consumption do not necessarily stand as points on a single line. Rather, they are different activities carried out by different social and cultural groups.

The collapse of the possibility if not indeed the desirability of a universal articulation of the human condition represents a most serious and important moral dilemma. An acceptance of the fates thrown up by the dialectic of reification means that groups and individuals will actually be consigned to fixed identities from which they might never be able to free themselves. Acceptance of the dialectic (its apprehension as if it is natural) means that groups will be fabricators or consumers for all time, without the chance of legitimate action to change their own destinies. It is likely that those identities might become so fixed that they might tend to come to exist as if by nature and they could therefore be the basis of strategies of exclusion and oppression. As such the possibility of the simultaneity of two articulations of the human condition raises the moral problem of how the division might be overcome rather than simply accepted as they way things have to be (or, more insidiously, as the way things ought to be).

To this extent then, Hannah Arendt is quite right to make a plea for the reconstitution of a universal human condition which would enable concern to be expressed about others on the basis of their humanity rather than on the basis of their group membership. The problem is one of working out how this reconstitution might be possible when the fourth dimension of consumption has to be added to the articulations of the human condition and when the reconstitution begins from a position of division rather than simple decline and fall. The question is how human moral universality can be constituted on a terrain which accepts and embodies the social and cultural plurality which makes us act as humans. One small way of doing this is to highlight the existential doubts and material insecurities which are involved in the situations of fabrication and consumption. One small way of making the case for action not dull acceptance is to show that the subject positions of fabrication and consumption have their own specific worries and that individual participation in any one of the two cannot at all be taken for granted for all time. These are not safe and stable houses in which humanity might be able to accommodate itself. They are in fact decidedly rickety.

Even though it is typified by pleasure and the evident satisfaction of the desires stimulated by commodity aesthetics, existence in terms of consumption is shaped by anxiety. A significant aspect of that anxiety takes the form of a kind of desperation. The point is that consumption is not at all inevitable. It is in fact contingent and dependent on material circumstances. The pleasures of the satisfaction of commodity-oriented and commodity-stimulated desires tend to collapse when and if the individual is made unemployed or turned into a more flexible 'human resource'. When that happens the confidence required for enjoyment tends to disappear along with the money and the financial security which enables the purchasing of things. A fine illustration of this situation has been provided by Michael Harrington. In his survey of poverty in the United States, Harrington talks about the fate of the old labour aristocracy of steel workers and car workers. These groups have a long background of economic security and they have often been amongst the most consumption-oriented groups. But Harrington points out that with the decline of the industries which employed them, these workers have been forced to confront not poverty as such but the threat of poverty. The confidence required for consumption is punctured and, instead, the steel workers who would aspire to be consumers are forced to confront uncertainty and contingency. With the steel workers, Harrington says that: 'We enter, then, a limbo, a place of in-between, where everyone is suddenly confronted with the frightening, totally unexpected prospect of being pushed down into poverty, and where, for some, that fear will become reality' (Harrington 1985: 40).

The importance of the point Harrington makes is that it demonstrates that the position of any individual or group within the spaces and experiences of consumption is not once and for all. It cannot be taken for granted since inclusion could easily become exclusion to the extent that material security is less than entirely predictable. For this reason then any group which thinks that it might have cause to doubt long-term security is likely to be more than a little desperate to gain satisfaction here and now (because satisfaction might be quite impossible tomorrow). Such groups are also very likely to want to protect what they define as 'theirs' from the actual or potential claims of those who are thereby defined and experienced as 'others'. The others become a pressing threat which has to be dealt with through strategies of exclusion, indifference and socially constructed incompetence. From the point of view of the threatened and fearful consumers, the others tend to be defined as groups which 'failed where so many others succeeded, and they must still prove that cruel fate, rather than their corrupt character, bears responsibility for the failure'. They are likely to be identified as 'a public menace, as their clamourings for help forebode new restrictions on all those who can do without help' (Bauman 1988: 93).

But even those who do not feel the threat of ejection from the spaces and positions of consumption have their experiences of consumption shaped and overwhelmed by anxiety. Here the anxiety is attributable to the hidden secret of commodity aesthetics; the moment of the attainment of beauty and consumer bliss never comes because what I have today is more than likely to be quite obsolete tomorrow. And in so far as the commodities of tomorrow are advertised today (in order to stimulate the demands which the supplier will therefore promise to meet) I am always living a few seconds after satisfaction might have been possible. (This situation is very nicely depicted by Georges Perec in his novel *Things*; see Perec 1990.)

However, despite the presence of these anxieties, it must be said that for the most part the groups which are defined by and structured around consumption tend to be fairly ready to accept their lot. Their experiences of the world and their attitudes towards it are generally representative of what John Kenneth Galbraith has called the culture of contentment (Galbraith 1992). According to Galbraith, in nations such as Britain and the United States it is possible to find what he calls a contented majority. This majority does not represent a majority of the entire population, but it does represent the majority of those individuals who participate in political processes (and so, therefore, the political process is structured in their favour): 'They rule under the rich cloak of democracy, a democracy in which the less fortunate do not participate. . . . They can be . . . very angry and very articulate about what seems to invade their state of self-satisfaction' (Galbraith 1992: 15). This contented majority is not socially or

71

occupationally coherent. It is largely made up by a mixture of professionals and the highly skilled working class who have a secure or double household income: 'Doing well, many wish to do better. Having enough, many wish for more. Being comfortable, many raise vigorous objection to that which invades comfort' (Galbraith 1992: 16). The contented majority experience 'no self-doubt in their present situation. The future for the contented majority is thought effectively within their personal command' (Galbraith 1992: 16–17).

Galbraith contends that this electoral majority is held together by the sharing of what amount to common cultural attitudes. This is the culture of contentment. Firstly, the culture of contentment is shaped by an 'affirmation that those who compose it are receiving their just deserts. What the individual member aspires to have and enjoy is the product of his or her personal virtue, intelligence and effort' (Galbraith 1992: 18). Secondly, the culture of contentment is shaped by a concern with short-term costs as opposed to possible long-term gains: 'The reason is readily evident. The long run may not arrive . . . the costs of today's action falls or could fall on the favored community; taxes could be increased. The benefits in the longer run may well be for others to enjoy' (Galbraith 1992: 20). One implication of this emphasis on the short term is that democracies which are dominated by the culture of contentment tend increasingly to be characterized by inadequate infrastructures and a commitment to the solution of environmental problems only when there is enough proof that actually there is an environmental threat to be resolved (and the proof will come tomorrow – always tomorrow). Thirdly, the culture of contentment takes a highly selective view of state action; the state is identified as something which ought to be rolled back except in those areas of social security or military expenditure which 'are strong supports to the comfort and security of the contented majority' (Galbraith 1992: 23). (An obvious example of this in Britain would be the relative ease with which state benefits to the poor have been cut back with nary a protest whilst tax relief on mortgages has been touched only very gingerly.) The fourth characteristic of the culture of contentment is 'the tolerance shown by the contented of great differentials in income' (Galbraith 1992: 26). Galbraith argues that the contented majority accepts the overwhelming wealth of some so that it can protect its own wealth from claims by the poor: 'The plush advantage of the very rich is the price the contented electoral majority pays for being able to retain what is less but what is still very good' (Galbraith 1992: 26).

According to Galbraith the contented electoral majority is able to develop and express this culture of contentment because its position is 'being supported and enhanced by the presence in the modern economy of a large, highly useful, even essential class that does not share in the agreeable existence of the favored community'. This class is what Galbraith calls the 'functional underclass' (Galbraith 1992: 29). Indeed: 'The economically fortunate, not excluding those who speak with greatest regret of the existence of this class, are heavily dependent on its presence' (Galbraith 1992: 31). The underclass is functional because 'the poor in our economy are needed to do the work that the more fortunate do not do and would find manifestly distasteful, even distressing' (Galbraith 1992: 33). In other words, the functional underclass fabricates the world and clears away the rubbish (these are both activities in relation to what is experientially defined as nature) so that the world can be enjoyed and experienced as ever more enchanted by the contented majority which seeks to protect and enjoy its consumption of things (in these terms then, the contented majority, and more broadly the culture of contentment, is based on the terrain of second nature).

Whereas the consumption-oriented groups seek pleasure in the possession and the doing of the beauties of commodity aesthetics, the fabrication-oriented groups seek to gain entry into the world of enchantment. As Zygmunt Bauman notes: 'Consumers are not enemies of the poor. . . . What the poor are after is a better hand, not a different card game' (Bauman 1988: 93). Whereas consumption is an activity which is structured largely around satisfaction in the here and now combined with a commitment to making sure that others cannot enjoy these things, fabrication stresses hard work today so that one might be allowed to be satisfied tomorrow.

Consequently, it might well be said that fabrication is an activity motivated by precisely the kind of inner-worldly asceticism which Weber saw as the heavy cloak which would come to weigh us all down. Weber wrote that: 'The Puritan wanted to work in a calling; we are forced to do so.' He went on to explain that: 'when asceticism was carried out of monastic cells into everyday life, and began to dominate worldly morality, it did its part in building the tremendous cosmos of the modern economic order' (Weber 1930: 181). The playing out of the dialectic of reification has meant that Weber was wrong to universalize this fate. He failed to recognize the possibility that some social and cultural groups might well be able to buy themselves out of the hard-nosed empiricism of fabrication and disenchantment. He failed to see that some groups might instead be able to buy into the enchanted world of the consuming of things which seem to appear as if from nowhere, as if by magic. 'The Protestant Ethic' is now the guiding principle of the fabricators and the poor; it has a limited applicability to the activities, projects and the experiences of those social and cultural groups which are shaped by and concerned with consumption. They tend to exist solely in terms of the 'Spirit of Capitalism'.

The connection which Weber forged between the 'Protestant Ethic' and the 'Spirit of Capitalism' has been dismantled with the establishment and the consolidation of the division between fabrication (and the fabricators) and consumption (and the consumers). However, both fabrication and consumption are similar to the extent that they both represent modes of doing. They are activities which are structured around an identical assumption that in the first instance, 'man's thirst for knowledge could be assuaged only after he had put his trust into the ingenuity of his hands'. Indeed: 'The point was not that truth and knowledge were no longer important, but that they could be won only by "action" and not by contemplation' (Arendt 1958: 263). Within the situation of fabrication, that doing revolves around the connected activities of making and the practice of violence in relation to nature (both first and second). Within the situation of consumption that doing revolves around the search in the enchanted spaces for the commodities which will bring about the moment of absolute consumer bliss. To this extent then both fabrication and consumption can be understood as attitudes of tactility in relation to the things of the world. They share a concentration on tactility because they are both dependent upon the active use of senses on the part of the individual. The tactility is literal in the case of fabrication (a literal 'hands on' approach to the things of the world) but it is rather more metaphorical in the case of consumption (here, the tactility is a rather more sensual and emotional kind of touching).

In these relationships, there can be no space or place for contemplation. Indeed, contemplation (and possibly even the contemplator) becomes untrustworthy. Even though commodity aesthetics create a situation in which image precedes object, nevertheless they also create a situation in which image stimulates such keen and desperate desires that the eventual appearance of the commodity can only lead to a degree of disappointment (although of course commodity aesthetics operate in such a way that I blame the disappointment on my own incompetence and not on the thing itself). Commodity aesthetics separate the image which is contemplated from the object which is actively engaged with. Similarly, fabrication is an attitude which alters nature in accordance with the dictates of a plan which is liable to alteration at short notice (and so to some extent fabrication is always an activity in the service of the ultimate goal which has just been repudiated). In both situations, things might be different than they appear to be: 'Nothing indeed could be less trustworthy for acquiring knowledge and approaching truth than passive observation or mere contemplation. In order to be certain one had to make sure, and in order to know one had to do' (Arendt 1958: 264). (Clearly the process of disenchantment which Weber explored can also be included within this phrase; it too leads to doing and action as the only possible ways of making sure since all intellectual certainties can be taken apart and demolished.)

As such, doing and action in relation to things become the highest if not the sole possible meanings of what it is to be human. Indeed, contemplation ceases to be free in relation to the mundane world of everyday relationships (it ceases to be able to be borne on the wings of flights of fancy) and instead it becomes a blindly pragmatic servant of the dialectic of reification. Hannah Arendt makes much the same point in her own terminology when she says that through the increasing emphasis on activity, 'doing was the ultimate meaning for the sake of which contemplation was to be performed. . . . Contemplation itself became altogether meaningless' (Arendt 1958: 265). But without contemplation, without the *vita contemplativa*, it is hard to know how there might be any basis upon which it might be possible to propose any kind of a critique of the social and cultural implications and requirements of the dialectic of reification.

The dialectic of reification creates a most ambivalent situation.

Never has the *vita contemplativa* been so needed. Never has the *vita contemplativa* been so impossible. The subjects of the dialectic of reification have been stunned by the very worlds they fabricate and consume.

4

LOOKING AND LISTENING

The *Oxford English Dictionary* establishes that the word 'quiet' is derived from the Latin root *quies* which means rest and repose. The *Dictionary* says that quiet can be defined as a condition which is marked by 'the absence of all strife, bustle, stir or com- motion; also, free from noise or uproar, silent, still' (*OED*). As such, the word implies both physical stillness (the rest of repose) and the making or the hearing of no noise (the rest of silence). Quiet is both an environmental condition and a state of mind. In both cases quiet implies the situation of a kind of peace. It is a relative state.

According to Hannah Arendt quiet is the precondition of the *vita contemplativa*. And it would seem to be likely that she means to use the word quiet in both its environmental and its emotional senses. But for Arendt quiet is not just a situation we might or might not find ourselves in. For her, quiet is also something like a mode of being of the self. More than just an environmental circumstance, quiet is also how the individual feels. Quiet is who and what we are as much as it is where we are. Yet the probability that Arendt uses the word quiet in terms of a double meaning rather has to be guessed at; the identification of the possibility is based on a reading of intent which it might not be unreasonable to impute to Arendt rather than explicit and clear statements. The problem is that even though the condition of quiet is very import- ant to her analysis of the human condition Arendt does not really define what the word means for her purposes. She does not define the word except in so far as she is able to establish it as something like the other to what might consequently be inter- preted as the un-quiet of the *vita activa* (Arendt 1958: 15–18). In this way, if the *vita activa* is un-quiet and if for Arendt the *vita activa* involves the activities of labour, work, action and, in all, a general doing of violence to nature, then logically the *vita contemplativa* must be distinct from the activities and violence of the *vita activa*. It must be identical with, and it must have as its precondition, a certain quiet.

Arendt is evidently in no doubt that quiet can only be discussed and even imagined as a relational condition or situation. Quiet is not an absolute state of being in and for itself. Quiet is nothing other than the condition of the absence of noise. To this extent the category of quiet might seem to be susceptible to little more than a brief exercise in the analysis of the structure of language and the importance of binary oppositions in classifications of the order of things. Yet there can be little doubt that Arendt does something rather more than simply establish a narrative opposition between quiet and un-quiet.

The whole drift of *The Human Condition* suggests quite forcefully that with her comments on quiet Arendt is trying to go some way towards providing a sociological account of the conditions of possibility of contemplation. (Arendt needs to identify contemplation as an activity which exists in a complex of social and cultural relationships so that she can develop her story of decline and fall which contains the important theme of the subordination of contemplating to doing.) What all of this means is that within the framework set up by Arendt's account of *The Human Condition*, contemplation is not a human activity which occurs naturally and of its own accord. It is an activity which has social and cultural environmental preconditions. Arendt makes it plain that contemplation has to be understood as an achievement. It is not something which is necessarily and inevitably inscribed in or permitted by social and cultural relationships.

Arendt rather tends to imply that contemplation is a mental activity with physical inactivity. It is a thinking which requires barriers between itself and the un-quiet of the fabrication carried out in the mundane relationships of the *vita activa*. Without that objective barrier (without that zone of objectivity), contemplation could not occur because it would be indistinguishable from everything else. Indeed, without the possibility of distinguishing itself from everything else contemplation could not possibly know itself actually to be contemplation (and contemplation needs at least a measure of this self-knowledge if it is to be able to go on as an identifiable activity). Arendt establishes contemplation as something precious and delicate (if you will forgive that pass into the pastoral) which has to be protected and defended. As soon as it is opened up to the assaults of un-quiet, contemplation withers.

The framework of Arendt's analysis of the *vita contemplativa* is not terribly new. There is little about its structure which is specific to Arendt herself. Certainly, the way Arendt locates and diagnoses the activity and fate of contemplation in terms of a general reflection on the human condition is original (although of course the narrative structure of decline and fall is fairly conventional), but her account has its anchor firmly tied to the ground provided in St Thomas Aquinas's *Summa Theologiae* (Aquinas 1989). (For Arendt's own awareness of her use of Aquinas, see Arendt 1958: 303. Arendt is also heavily indebted to Aristotle and Augustine. But at least as far as the discussion of the *vita contemplativa* is concerned perhaps the debt to Aquinas is the most glaring. After all, and in any case, Aquinas can be understood to some extent to represent a synthesis of Aristotle with Augustine.)

Aquinas was in absolutely no doubt about the importance of contemplation. He saw it as the surest road to the happiness which is 'another name for God . . . men become happy by receiving a share in God's happiness' (Aquinas 1989: 176). According to Aquinas, contemplation is a rather more reliable means than action of attaining happiness. This is because action can be broken into a number of specific and particular activities or occupations, whereas contemplation requires a single and ongoing concentration. Action is a series of small steps whereas contemplation requires sustained commitment. For Aquinas, 'a life of action, occupied with many things, offers less happiness than a life of contemplation, engaged in the one activity of gazing at truth' (Aquinas 1989: 176).

Action is oriented towards the achievement of specific and discrete goals whereas contemplation is oriented towards the achievement of a universal end. Contemplation is the mode of being which provides the surest guarantees of happiness and it is, therefore, something towards which the individual ought always to be open. And Aquinas believes that the individual can in fact always be ready for contemplation. Indeed, even if an individual is not actually engaged in contemplation at any given moment in time it is nevertheless the case that, 'because he is ever open and ready and turns his very breaks in contemplation, due to sleep or natural business, to its service, his contemplation seems as if it were unbroken' (Aquinas 1989: 176–177). Even when we are not contemplating we are, therefore, ready to contemplate, replenishing our resources for renewed and recommitted effort.

Aquinas was perfectly prepared to turn this argument into the basis of a hierarchic conception of the relationship between activity and contemplation. The hierarchy is established on the foundation that: 'Man's highest activity engages his highest power with its highest object. Man's intelligence is his highest power, and its highest object the good that is God, an object of contemplative not practical intelligence' (Aquinas 1989: 177). What Aquinas calls the 'practical' is less able than contemplation to lead to happiness, not only because it upholds no universal and ultimate truth but also because it does not engage what is highest about humanity. Rather, since the 'practical mind pursues knowledge not for its own but for action's sake, and actions in turn pursue goals' then 'practical knowledge and the life of action with which it is concerned cannot be our ultimate goal' (Aquinas 1989: 177).

Aquinas's position leads to a very definite attitude towards the things which are found in the material world: 'The partial happiness of this life does not consist in having external goods, but requires them as tools to serve that exercise of man's powers and skills and virtues in which this life's happiness does consist' (Aquinas 1989: 180). This identification of material things out there (objects) as tools in the service of the contemplation which occurs in here (subjectively), even extends to the interpretation and the status of other human beings. Indeed, 'the happy man' in this life needs friends, 'not for their external usefulness, since his happiness is from within, nor for pleasure, since his perfect pleasure comes from the activity of virtue, but as contributing to that activity itself' (Aquinas 1989: 180). Aquinas makes it even more plain that friends are tools like any other material things which exist objectively when he says that: 'the companionship of friends is not strictly necessary . . . to the perfect happiness of our heavenly home, where a man is completely and wholly fulfilled in God, yet the companionship of friends enhances that happiness' (Aquinas 1989: 180).

Aquinas adds detail to his discussion when he distinguishes between contemplation as a way of life and contemplation as a state of life. What Aquinas does with his distinction is stress the extent to which contemplation is an activity carried out by individuals or groups which have to thereby occupy certain specific subject positions.

According to Aquinas contemplation is a way of life to the extent that the pursuit of truth by the individual represents a property or quality of humanity which is 'the activity specially appropriate to it on which it is bent: plants feed and propagate, animals feel and move, men understand and act rationally' (Aquinas 1989: 451). Humanity is driven towards the attempt to discover the truth. Even though the movement in a sentence from the propagation of plants to the understanding and rationality of humanity might imply that such understanding and rationality stand as innate aspects of a human nature, Aquinas goes on to argue that this way of life (here, then, the word 'way' can be understood as a road which is taken to lead to a definite destination – truth) is self-motivated and, in the first instance, self-chosen: 'the contemplative life is a life of mental activity, but what stimulates us to live in this way is our will which activates all our powers including mind' (Aquinas 1989: 451). According to Aquinas, this contemplative life requires the quiet of repose which can only be found through a subjective distanciation from physical and material activity. Indeed, Aquinas was quite sure that 'as the active life occupies itself with external activities it clearly hinders the contemplative life, because one can't at the same time be occupied with external activity and free for contemplation of God' (Aquinas 1989: 453).

Aquinas is in no doubt that the contemplative way of life, 'is hindered both by strong passions which distract our attention from mind to sense, and by external worries' (Aquinas 1989: 451). Contemplation requires an ability to subordinate, if not indeed entirely overcome, the demands of the senses (and of course this includes sensual gratification such as sexual pleasure): 'No person living this life can contemplate the very substance of God, if by living this present life we mean actually using our bodily senses' (Aquinas 1989: 452). Here then it is clear that the body with its sensual desires and pleasures tends to stands as something to be overcome if the contemplative way of life is to be possible and if it is to be able to retain sight of the fact that, for Aquinas: 'The goal activity of the contemplative life is the contemplation of truth' (Aquinas 1989: 452). The senses mortify contemplation and therefore themselves require mortification.

Aquinas asserts and justifies a belief that the contemplative way of life (which is more or less identical with Arendt's *vita contemplativa*) is preferable to the active way of life (Arendt's *vita activa*) through a citation of the authority of Aristotle. Aquinas uses Aristotle to justify two claims. Firstly, contemplation is preferable to activity because 'It agrees with what is best in man, his mind, and with its most appropriate objects, the things the mind can understand; whereas the active life is busy with external things' (Aquinas 1989: 453). Secondly, contemplation is preferable because it is concerned with God whereas the active life is only concerned with human affairs. (Arendt turns contemplation back towards this world and thus reinserts it into a single order of things along with the *vita activa*. In that way she is able to offer a reason for her refusal to establish a hierarchy between contemplation and activity.) For Aquinas drawing on Aristotle, the active life is only seen as preferable in the case of direct physical need and to the extent that it develops some of the discipline required by and for contemplation. As Aquinas puts it: 'inasmuch as the active life integrates and controls the interior emotions it fosters the contemplative life, which would be hindered by disordered emotion' (Aquinas 1989: 453).

Whereas contemplation as a way of life stresses what the individual wills to become, contemplation as a state of life stresses what the individual actually is in the here and now. If the way of life emphasizes achievement then the state of life emphasizes ascription. As Aquinas puts it: 'We don't count as a state of life any condition that is external or easily changed: being rich or poor, a dignitary or an ordinary citizen.' On the contrary: 'A state of life implies some obligation, some area in which a man is or is not his own master, and that in some permanent way, not transiently or trivially' (Aquinas 1989: 453). In sum then, a state of life is defined 'by some stable situation persons are in' (Aquinas 1989: 453).

The interpretation of contemplation as a state of life is less concerned with the whys and wherefores of contemplation than it is concerned to emphasize the precise social and cultural settings and situations in which the activity might be able to take place. For Aquinas, these situations are religious houses which 'should be established for preaching and for other activities directed at the welfare of souls' (Aquinas 1989: 465). Within these institutions, the main and indeed only really acceptable activity is study in the service of contemplation. After all, for Aquinas study 'promotes the contemplative life directly by enlightening the mind and indirectly by removing the dangers of contemplation' (Aquinas 1989: 465). Study is a situation of quiet because it plays a part in 'restraining cravings of the flesh and desire for riches, and teaching obedience' (Aquinas 1989: 465). But study is also a situation of quiet because it might lead to solitude: 'Solitude is a tool of contemplation, but not of the active life, whether that life be physically or spiritually active, unless the solitude be temporary like Christ's' (Aquinas 1989: 466). Any being with others consequently is only a training ground for absolute solitude (this point connects with Aquinas's depiction of friends as tools): 'Solitude suits the contemplative who is already perfect, but life in community is necessary for training in perception.' The highest point of contemplation is represented in the absolute quiet and absolute solitude of the hermit: 'What is already perfect surpasses what is only working towards perfection, so the life of a hermit, if properly lived, surpasses life in community' (Aquinas 1989: 466).

What Aquinas does very well, although perhaps not explicitly or intentionally, is show that contemplation has social and cultural conditions of existence. These conditions of existence revolve around the ability to choose and then develop a rational mode of subjectivity as well as the existence of the spatial situations in which contemplation might be carried out free from the temptations of the flesh or worldly riches. These conditions are all contained within the image of quiet. That quiet is both experiential and situational. It is experiential because it concerns the free choice and living out of the demands of the way of life. It is situational because it concerns the firm foundations beyond doubt within which that choice is practised in terms of a state of life.

Perhaps the main shortcoming of Aquinas from a sociological point of view is that he pulls together the experience and the situation of quiet rather too much. Even though he is at least implicitly aware that the way of life and the state of life involve different kinds of quiet, he nevertheless tends to subsume these two particular definitions within a general definition. With Aquinas, experience and situation tend to come together because way of life and state of life also tend to come together in the shape of specific individuals or communities practising religious modes of subjectivity. Aquinas's reasons for this direct connection are fairly obvious. The pulling together of the different kinds of quiet means that Aquinas is able to develop a system which is, in its own terms, total and totalizing. He was, after all, trying to develop a comprehensive system of knowledge (and implicitly a comprehensive system of the organization of the religious life) which would establish a single and therefore orthodox route to God. Had the different quiets of the way of life and of the state of life not been brought together, Aquinas's system would have foundered on the reef of plurality; there would have been no single truth around which his discourse could have been constructed.

Perhaps Aquinas's account of contemplation still holds good for those who enter into religious houses. But perhaps with its secularization, Aquinas's account was also broken up along the line of distinction between the experience and the situation of contemplation. And Aquinas's account has indeed been subject to a process of secularization. The obvious instance of this process of secularization is the ease with which Hannah Arendt is able to develop a thoroughly Godless analysis of the human condition which has built within it themes from the *Summa Theologiae*. From a strictly sociological point of view it can be argued that the preconditions of contemplation which Aquinas identifies remain of analytic usefulness even though the experience and the situation of quiet might now tend to represent two different conditions of social and cultural relationships.

As such I want to propose that sociologically, the fairly straightforward (and certainly single) division between quiet and un-quiet which Aquinas and thereafter Arendt are so keen to draw has tended to collapse. The tendency towards collapse has its roots in the assaults which are directed towards the experience and the situation of quiet by the simultaneously literal and metaphorical un-quiet of contemporary social and cultural relationships. I want to try to substantiate that proposition by arguing that the situation of quiet is represented by Galbraith's culture of contentment which is, however, partially subject to experiences of discontent (experiences of un-quiet in relation to the quiet centre of the culture of contentment). Meanwhile, the experience of quiet has collapsed for the somewhat simple (but woefully underresearched) fact that ours is a very noisy world.

I am very aware of the rather huge leap in the argument from Aquinas to Galbraith. But perhaps the leap is not as ludicrous as it might at first seem. Firstly, it can be justified on the grounds that perhaps we have not entirely left Aquinas behind. Certainly, I have not discussed Aquinas for antiquarian purposes. On the contrary, it is possible to suggest that the connections Aquinas makes between quiet as a situation and an experience and the contemplative life continues to run through contemporary social and cultural relationships. The dominant social and cultural narratives about the 'creative life' (which can be understood as the *vita contemplativa* turned thoroughly secular and turned out of any necessary institutional location) commonly tend to emphasize quiet of some sort (and so it can be speculated – although there is not at all the space or intention to pursue the speculation here – that the myths of the 'tortured artist' all emphasize the assaults of experiential, existential or environmental un-quiet of one sort or another). Secondly, Aquinas is useful because, whatever the status of his discussion of contemplation (whether it is 'true' or fiction, demystification or mythication), it provides something like a benchmark against which it might be possible to develop some kind of critique of contemporary relationships, institutions and arrangements. Irrespective of its truth or otherwise, Aquinas's account can be used in order to do something more than simply describe or dully accept what currently passes as being necessary. As such, it is exactly the jarring between Aquinas and some more contemporary commentator like Galbraith which is of interest and importance to me.

When Galbraith defines his culture of contentment he is actually talking about what amounts to a social and cultural situation of metaphorical quiet. This quiet is in important ways a product of the accommodation of ideas to the exigencies of contentment. According to Galbraith, certain economic narratives have emerged which claim to offer some legitimacy and erstwhile necessity to the culture of contentment. He suggests that a narrative which bolsters the position and interests of the contented 'need not be subject to serious empirical proof . . . it need not even be seriously persuasive . . . it is the availability and not the substance that serves' (Galbraith 1992: 97–98). In my terms, this means that the culture has been given the possibility of not having to face doubt about its own status; its foundations have become things about which the contented can be quiet. According to Galbraith, economics has served the culture of contentment by lending it a gloss of necessity in three ways.

Firstly, economics has offered a justification for a limitation on government activity (the culture of contentment has an interest in the 'rolling back' of the state because smaller states evidently require smaller tax revenues). Galbraith argues that this support for contentment was derived from a somewhat partial reading of Adam Smith. Galbraith implies that Smith was useful because he lent an aura of the weight of tradition to contemporary concerns and policies. Smith was also an advantageous figure to cite because so few people have actually read his *Wealth of Nations*. As Galbraith puts the matter: 'It is perhaps unfortunate that few, perhaps none, who so cited Adam Smith had read his great book' (Galbraith 1992: 99). Smith's book was interpreted as providing reasons for a state which ostensibly adopted a hands-off policy towards economic activity and the supposedly moral operation of the free market. The point is of course that a state which follows such a *laissez-faire* policy will not make any effort to undermine the position of the contented. It will have no justification nor cause to do so. Indeed, the very existence of the culture of contentment, as of the contented themselves, is more likely to be held up as the clinching proof of the moral and beneficial operation of the market system.

Secondly, economics has sought to 'find social justification for the untrammeled, uninhibited pursuit and possession of wealth' (Galbraith 1992: 96–97). This justification has two parts: firstly, the claim that the rich need to be given the motivation to get richer whilst the poor need to have welfare provision removed in order to force them to pull themselves out of poverty by their own bootstraps (Galbraith 1992: 101–102); secondly, the claim that the tax burden on the richer members of the population could be reduced without having an adverse impact on the overall revenue of the state (Galbraith 1992: 103–104). The point of this aspect of the economic accommodation to the culture of contentment is precisely that it means that the contented will see a relatively reduced proportion of their income being taken away in the form of direct taxation. Such a reduction in taxation is justified on the grounds that it emancipates the wealth creators from the state and thus means that whatever extra they might earn through their own efforts will go straight into their own pockets. Indeed, the tax burden on individuals allegedly can be reduced without having a negative impact on overall state revenue because, it is argued, if the tax burden on individuals is reduced, more individuals will be encouraged to pursue wealth creation and, therefore, there will be a global increase in the number of the wealthy. More people can pay less (or certainly no more) each in order to give the same, or even a slightly increased, global increase on tax revenue. Meanwhile, the poor are treated in a completely opposite way; just as the contented are identified as contented because of their own hard work, so the poor are identified and constructed as poor precisely because of their own sloth and indolence. As such, the poor have to be put in a situation where the state will not necessarily 'provide' for them. This argument leads into the third aspect of what Galbraith calls the economic accommodation to contentment.

Thirdly, there has been a requirement to challenge any sense of 'public responsibility for the poor'. Galbraith contends that the members of his functional underclass 'must, in some very real way, be seen as the architects of their own fate. If not, they could be, however marginally, on the conscience of the comfortable.' Put another way, there could be an experience of un-quiet amongst the contented (or at least a lingering doubt could be placed over the quiet of their contentment): 'There could be a disturbing feeling, of unease, even guilt' (Galbraith 1992: 97). These chances of disturbance were lessened by the emergence of the work of Charles A. Murray which argues, according to Galbraith's gloss, that: 'the poor are impoverished and are kept in poverty by the public measures, particularly the welfare payments, that are meant to rescue them from their plight'. Indeed, in this view of the world: 'The help becomes a substitute for the personal initiative and effort that would bring true escape' (Galbraith 1992: 106). In other words, there is something very much like the construction from the point of view of the culture of contentment of the problem of the culture of dependency. What this construction of the other to contentment means is that the poor cease to be a problem about which the contented need worry. They become their own problem and stand in urgent need of eviction from their dependency on 'state handouts'. As Galbraith says, this strategy of blaming the poor and the state for poverty has the practical implication (if the narrative is translated into policy) that: 'The poor would be off the conscience of the comfortable and, a point of even greater importance, off the federal budget and tax system' (Galbraith 1992: 106–107).

Galbraith says that these three narratives came together in the

1980s to constitute what was called 'supply side economics'. 'So far as it has specific content, this meant that economic policy would henceforth be focused . . . on those that, by rewarding initiative and therewith production, expanded the economy by increasing the supply of goods and services.' Consequently: 'the rich needed the spur of more money, the poor the spur of their own poverty' (Galbraith 1992: 107).

What Galbraith sees as the reconciliation of strands of economics to the interests and aspirations of the culture of contentment can easily be identified as a situation of metaphorical quiet. On the one hand the culture of contentment is a culture of quiet because its evident material security means that few if any questions need to be raised about how it might (or might not) be sustainable. To this extent the culture of contentment is not, because it does not need to be, at all reflexive. It does not need to think about its own conditions of existence. All it needs to do is make those conditions all the more stable. On the other hand, the culture of contentment can be identified as a situation of a kind of quiet because, in so far as what Galbraith calls the 'economic accommodation' succeeds, then contentment itself becomes second nature. It becomes something which exists as if of necessity, and as if of its own accord. Contentment becomes the just dessert of the relatively affluent.

Galbraith believes that the contented do have strong responsibilities and obligations in relation to the poor but, on the other hand, his analysis of the culture of contentment gives him few if any reasons to believe that the contented will realize these moral responsibilities for themselves. The contented have to be made to realize moral obligations towards the underclass. But that realization might not involve anything much more than enlightened self-interest. Galbraith notes that the underclass might come to stand as a direct and immediate threat to the maintenance of contentment.

But it can be suggested that the threat of revolt and violence which the underclass might present will never be able to scale the walls from outside to inside the culture of contentment. It might never be able to enter into the sensibilities and the consciousness of the contented. This is for two reasons. Firstly, the underclass will be kept at arm's length by means of the wealthy buying private security services and provision. This would involve: 'a resort by the contented in the larger cities to a *laager* mentality –

the hiring of personal, neighborhood or apartment security guards or the escape to presumptively safe suburbs' (Galbraith 1992: 171). Secondly, the underclass will be kept at arm's length through increasingly rigorous and draconian surveillance. Indeed, Galbraith contends that if urban discontent and crime increases it is quite likely that it, 'will be attributed not to the social situation but to the inferior, even criminal, disposition of the people involved' (Galbraith 1992: 172). Urban violence ostensibly perpetrated by the underclass will be explained away on the grounds of their innate evil. Urban violence and unrest will be held by the speakers on behalf of contentment to have nothing whatsoever to do with social and cultural relationships. In this way, the violence is turned into a property of first nature which requires discipline and, even better if at all possible, extirpation.

According to Galbraith then, the culture of contentment is able to bolster itself against attack from without. The culture of contentment is able to respond to any event from outside simply by turning its back on it: 'it is not in the nature of contentment that such eventualities, however persuasively described, be other than ignored'. Indeed: 'Contentment sets aside that which, in the longer view, disturbs contentment; it holds firmly to the thought that the long run may never come' (Galbraith 1992: 173). This might well be true in situational terms. The culture of contentment might well be able to avoid having to face the consequences of its own selfishness. It might well be able to avoid having to confront the material presences of those individuals who are consigned to the underclass. But perhaps Galbraith rather tends to overstate the homogeneity of the experience of contentment. If attention is paid to what contentment means and involves at an experiential level, then it is possible to identify the emergence of a paradox. The paradox is that even though certain social and cultural groups are situated within a culture of contentment, the individuals in those groups are, in fact, unlikely to experience themselves as being especially content. It is likely that their experiences of self and the world will be determined not by contentment but by a niggling sense of discontent; not by quiet but by un-quiet.

Part of that experience of un-quiet revolves around the possibility that any given individual is liable to be thrown out of the culture of contentment when and if she or he is made redundant. In these terms then a position within the boundaries of the culture is entirely contingent and dependent upon forces over which the individual has little or no control (economic forces which evidently operate as laws and which strike as if like nature). But the un-quiet also operates at a far less dramatic level than that demonstrated by such events as unemployment. The un-quiet is actually an inevitable aspect of the culture of contentment. The point is of course that to a significant degree, contentment is demonstrated through practices of consumption; the individual is content in so far as she or he is able to buy private security provision, private medical care and so forth. Equally, the individual is content to the extent that she or he is in a position to be able to buy the commodities which promise a way out of want and need. But as Haug (1986) shows with his account of commodity aesthetics, the individual who practises consumption can never achieve the final state of contentment. Commodities promise too much and deliver too little for them to be the basis of any definite and definitive sense of self (and of course it is precisely the disjuncture between the promise and the actuality which in part makes sure that capitalist relationships are amenable to reproduction). Contentment involves the doing of consumption and, therefore, it cannot possibly be the foundation of any being of contentment. (It is also possible to diagnose the problems associated with commodity aesthetics in terms derived directly from Aquinas; they cannot lead to happiness because they revolve around purely sensual pleasures and around the desires of the flesh which needs to be mortified if the true happiness of God is going to be approached.) Consequently, if contentment is a situation of quiet then it is purchased at the expense of the impossibility of any escape from the experience of un-quiet.

Yet un-quiet is not simply an experience in the metaphorical sense. It is much more than that; un-quiet is an experience in a very literal sense too. We all experience un-quiet in so far as ours is a very noisy world. And it is not unreasonable to speculate that the physical, material, sensual un-quiet of noise also has a profound effect on the possibility of contemplation and, much more broadly, upon how individuals experience the worlds they (we) inhabit. The noisiness of this world is immensely difficult to write about. It is difficult to write about noise because writing (and often reading) are quiet activities and activities of quiet, and also because noise is a quality of the environment into which the individual is born and, therefore, likely to be fairly deaf towards. It is difficult for us to have any great sense of how noisy our world might be precisely because we are unable to abstract ourselves from it. There is no Archimedean point of perfect quiet from which the un-quiet of noise might be known (the most we can have are day trips to states of relative quiet).

Johan Huizinga recognized this problem of how it might be possible to understand the relative states of silence and noise. At the very beginning of *The Waning of the Middle Ages*, he comments that there are some things about that period which we cannot really comprehend (Huizinga 1955: 9). One of those things is quiet. Huizinga suggests that in the Middle Ages: 'The contrast between silence and sound . . . was more strongly marked than it is in our lives. The modern town hardly knows . . . the effect of . . . a single distant cry' (Huizinga 1955: 10). Accordingly, Huizinga believes, life in the Middle Ages was experienced far more starkly than life is experienced now: 'All things presenting themselves to the mind in violent contrasts and impressive forms, lent a tone of excitement and of passion to everyday life.' Emotional life also tended to move between stark opposites (Huizinga 1955: 10). (Compare this story to the one told by Elias; he reaches similar conclusions by a different route; Elias 1978.) The subtext of Huizinga's account is that contemporary relationships are much more mediocre than the social and cultural relationships of the Middle Ages. We live our lives much more in the balanced middle. Our lives are less dramatic, less profound, less emotional. But they are all the more stable for that.

Huizinga's story would suggest that contemporary social and cultural relationships are therefore likely to be experienced in terms of a mixture of boredom and certainty. However, perhaps the changing configurations of noise have in part led to a situation in which we are, in fact, almost perpetually confused, bewildered, exhausted and drained. This is a possibility which is opened up by Georg Simmel. He explores some of the consequences of noise for how individuals experience the world. But he also stresses that the experience of noise (that is, listening) is not a sensual apprehension which exists in glorious isolation. Simmel stresses the point that individuals sensually experience the world through a combination of listening with looking. Simmel also locates the problems of looking and listening in specific social and cultural and spatial sites. He ties his analysis to

91

the problems and possibilities of urban relationships and arrangements (Simmel 1969: 360).

Simmel contends that: 'Social life in the large city as compared with the towns shows a great preponderance of occasions to see rather than to hear people' (Simmel 1969: 360). He gives two explanations for this state of affairs. Firstly, life in cities is about seeing more than it is about hearing because, 'the person in the town is acquainted with nearly all the people he meets. With these he exchanges a word or a glance, and their countenance represents to him not merely the visible but indeed the entire personality' (Simmel 1969: 360). In other words, in urban settings we all see a lot of other people who we know only to the extent that we frequently see them walking along the same streets we walk along ourselves. Consequently, for mundane purposes, the complete being of that other person is revealed and demonstrated in the rituals and restraints of public encounters. Secondly, Simmel explains the preponderance of looking over and above listening by emphasizing some of the implications of the technologies of contemporary urban life and relationships. As Simmel writes: 'Before the appearance of omnibuses, railroads, and street cars in the nineteenth century, men were not in a situation where for periods of minutes or hours they could or must look at each other without talking to one another' (Simmel 1969: 360). Here then, Simmel is pointing to one of the most characteristic aspects of urban life; we frequently find ourselves on public transport trying to make sense of the person opposite who is looking at us, trying to make sense of us, but without actually talking and without actually getting caught looking. We see our fellow passengers but we do not hear them for the simple reason that there is in fact little or nothing to be heard. It is strange that Simmel did not highlight another reason for the preponderance of seeing over hearing on public transport. It is strange that he did not stress the point that public transport is frequently extremely noisy. Either the bus or train makes so much noise that we cannot hear a conversation or, alternatively, there might be so many conversations going on at the same time that it is impossible clearly to make out any single one of them.

These common urban encounters are of much more than descriptive or anecdotal importance. According to Simmel they can be used as ways of understanding the typical experiences and features of urban existence. In particular, the experiences of seeing others on streets and seeing not hearing others on public transport can be used as ways of appreciating the extent to which, in urban settings, all individuals are thrown into a world of noise and un-quiet which makes them all what Simmel calls 'deaf-mutes'. For Simmel, if we were all like the blind then the world would be able to make some kind of sense to us (because it would allow for certain kinds of metaphorical quiet). But he contends that because we are all like the deaf the world is nothing other than utterly perplexing and stressful. Ironically, when we are all metaphorically deaf (or perhaps it is better to say that when we are all deafened by the environments we inhabit), then the quiet of contemplation is quite impossible to find.

In order to justify these points (which of course I have begun to put into my own terminology by connecting them with the problem of quiet and un-quiet), Simmel explores what he takes to be the different ways in which the blind and the deaf respectively make sense of the other people they meet. Simmel identifies blindness as permitting a kind of rest and repose in the world. He writes that: 'For the blind, the other person is actually present only in the alternating periods of his utterances.' Indeed: 'The expression of the anxiety and unrest, the traces of all past events, exposed to view in the faces of men, escape the blind' (Simmel 1969: 360). The reason for this 'peaceful and calm disposition' (Simmel 1969: 360) is that, 'in general, what we see of a man will be interpreted by what we hear from him, while the opposite is more unusual'. Consequently: 'the one who sees, without hearing, is much more perplexed, puzzled, and worried, than the one who hears without seeing' (Simmel 1969: 360). And the point is precisely that the relationships, arrangements and technologies of urban existence are such that we are indeed all like individuals who see without hearing.

The noises of urban existence deafen us all. We are fated to live in un-quiet environments which allow for neither contemplation nor for individuals who are quiet in their relationship with themselves. The un-quiet environment produces and permits only un-quiet slumbers. Simmel was in no doubt that 'The greater perplexity which characterizes the person who only sees, as contrasted with the one who only hears' (Simmel 1969: 360) has immediate and immense emotional consequences. It leads to 'the lack of orientation in the collective life, the sense of utter lone-someness, and the feeling that the individual is surrounded on all sides by closed doors' (Simmel 1969: 361).

The individual responds to this environment and experience of un-quiet perplexity by withdrawing into him or her self. To this extent it is quite clear that Simmel's diagnosis of the city dweller as someone who is deaf or deafened is of a part with his somewhat more famous account of 'The Metropolis and Mental Life'. In that essay he provides a slightly different route to the conclusion that the inhabitants of urban environments tend to draw in upon themselves and thus emotionally withdraw from the generality of others. In that essay, Simmel famously distinguishes between the blasé and the reserved attitudes. He identifies these attitudes as products of urban relationships and arrangements and psychological defence mechanisms in relation to the urban swirl.

The blasé and reserved attitudes are not adopted by individuals through an act of purposive choice. They are not intentional. Rather they are emotional responses to material social and cultural processes, experiences and situations without which a continuous sense of self would be very seriously prejudiced. Neither are the blasé and reserved attitudes like cloaks which can be thrown off as soon as the individual leaves the city streets and instead walks amongst the harebells. If Simmel is right, these attitudes play an absolutely crucial role in the formation and maintenance of individuals in urban environments. Indeed, they are so important that any individual who is removed from the urban environments which stimulate the blasé and reserved attitudes is likely to feel completely lost and bewildered. The city generates attitudes which take such a deep hold in the emotional and existential constitution of the self that if the experiences to which they respond are absent then the individual is unlikely to be able to make much sense of the different worlds she or he finds him or her self in. The individual produced by the urban environment needs the un-quiet of the city in order to be able to operate. Quiet as such becomes something incomprehensible and, quite possibly, even terrifying (at the very least, quiet is likely to be experienced as utterly boring if it is not contained within the clearly demarcated boundaries of a holiday).

Simmel is sure that: 'There is perhaps no psychic phenomenon which has been so unconditionally reserved to the metropolis as has the blasé attitude' (Simmel 1950: 413). The blasé attitude is identified by Simmel as a direct response to the excesses of stimulation which the urban environment forces upon the individual. It is so much a part of the second nature of the inhabitant of the city that 'every metropolitan child shows [it] when compared with children of quieter and less changeable milieus' (Simmel 1950: 414). The blasé attitude amounts to an environmentally generated incapacity on the part of the individual either to think or respond to new sensations in a way which those sensations warrant. In the city the individual sees and hears so much going on that 'through the rapidity and contradictoriness of their changes, more harmless impressions force such violent responses, tearing the nerves so brutally hither and thither that their last reserves of strength are spent'. Indeed, 'if one remains in the same milieu they have no time to gather new strength. An incapacity thus emerges to react to new sensations with the appropriate energy' (Simmel 1950: 414). Specifically, for the individual made by the city everything merges into a flat monotony towards which the only reasonable reaction, and certainly the only sustainable reaction, is one of complete indifference: 'This does not mean that the objects are not perceived . . . but rather that the meaning and differing values of things, and thereby the things themselves, are experienced as insubstantial' (Simmel 1950: 414).

However, the individual is only able to preserve him or her self in the face of this tendency towards the blasé and the apprehension of insubstantiality to the extent that she or he is able to develop the emotional and psychological defence mechanism of reserve. Simmel speculates that without the withdrawal from others which is implied by the attitude of reserve, the individual would be existentially torn apart. 'If so many inner reactions were responses to the continuous external contacts with innumerable people as are those in the small town . . . one would be completely atomized internally and come to an unimaginable psychic state' (Simmel 1950: 415). By pulling in on ourselves, we are able to keep ourselves together. Simmel observes that 'As a result of this reserve we frequently do not even know by sight those who have been our neighbors for years' (Simmel 1950: 415). One aspect of this reserve is likely to be the turning away of the gaze from the other person who is caught looking at us. And this looking away can almost be seen, for Simmel, as a harbinger of a collapse of social and cultural empathy between individuals.

According to Simmel: 'Of the special sense-organs, the eye has a uniquely sociological function.' The eye is so important because: 'The union and interaction of individuals is based upon mutual glances. This is perhaps the most direct and purest reciprocity which exists anywhere' (Simmel 1969: 358). This reciprocity of glances is 'direct and pure' because it implies a unity between individuals which exists independently of, and indeed prior to, any social and cultural status they might possess or roles they might perform. It is a reciprocity which is separate from any kind of social and cultural institutionalization or arrangement: 'This highest psychic reaction . . . in which the glances of eye to eye unite men, crystallizes into no objective structure; the unity which momentarily arises between two persons is present in the occasion and is dissolved in the function' (Simmel 1950: 358). Without this reciprocity of glances, social and cultural relationships would be made extremely unpredictable and, quite possibly, evacuated of any content which emphasizes the relevance of humans purely as humans (Simmel 1969: 358.) The problem is, however, that Simmel is easily able to identify sociological processes which imply a series of powerful challenges to this fleeting yet self-sufficient unity of individuals which is made in the 'mutual glance between persons, in distinction from the simple sight or observation of the other' (Simmel 1969: 358).

Certainly, the attitude of reserve would seem to represent a direct challenge to the reciprocity of glances which for Simmel is built on the principle that: 'By the glance which reveals the other, one discloses himself. By the same act in which the observer seeks to know the observed, he surrenders himself to be understood by the observer' (Simmel 1969: 358). Reserve means precisely that the individual will tend to try to refuse the glance of the general other. (Although this means that the individual is likely to pin ever greater and ever more impossible to achieve hopes upon the return of the glance from the specific other; from the beloved. It can be speculated that love as a relationship with a single other who is defined as wholly significant will increase in importance as the individual apprehends more and more individuals from whom the glance must be turned away, or who themselves turn away their glance.) Reserve causes a sense of shame which itself inspires the individual 'to look to the ground to avoid the glance of the other' (Simmel 1969: 358). The looking away means that the individual is able to hide him or her self from the interrogative glance of the other. It also means that the other will be unable to see that the individual does not really know what to do when a glance is reciprocated in a way which cannot be made completely and immediately meaningful by social and cultural arrangements.

Wolfgang Schivelbusch has explored one specific and very common instance of this situation in which individuals try to avoid making eye contact with each other. He has explored some of the relationships which take place in railway carriages. According to Schivelbusch, who quite explicitly takes his lead from Simmel, reading is such a popular practice on railway journeys precisely because it is a way of coming to terms with the presence of others who can be seen but not necessarily heard, others who can be seen looking at the individual but who try hard not to get caught looking. Schivelbusch believes that railway journeys are sources of embarrassment because, although all the passengers are forced to sit facing each other, they have absolutely nothing to say to one another (Schivelbusch 1980: 80). As such the meeting of glances causes only fear and un-quiet because it is likely to be interpreted as an intrusion more than as an invitation to discussion. Reading solves the existential and psychological problems which might thus arise: 'the perusal of reading matter is an attempt to replace the conversation that is no longer possible. Fixing one's eyes on a book or a newspaper, one is able to avoid the stare of the person sitting across the aisle' (Schivelbusch 1980: 80).

The point is that even though I might be able to explore the meaning of the other by looking at her or him, the other is able to do exactly the same to me. All of these glances imply a kind of knowledge which is quite incompatible with the strategies and frames of mind associated with the attitude of reserve. For Simmel: 'The glance in the eye of the other serves not only for me to know the other but also enables him to know me.' Consequently: 'Upon the line which unites the two eyes, it conveys to the other the real personality, the real attitude, and the real impulse' (Simmel 1969: 358–359). It reveals everything which reserve tries to keep firmly hidden from sight. Looking away frees me from you, but it also means that I am imprisoned in the existential prison of my own making. (It is not unreasonable to propose that the dialectic of reciprocity and paranoia which Simmel identifies in the sociological relationships of the glance is expressed in Sartre's analysis of the look in *Being and Nothingness*. See Sartre 1958: 252–302.)

The implication of Simmel's account of the reciprocity of the glance is a statement of the significance of the mutual recognition of faces in the construction of social and cultural bonds. In other words, Simmel is implying that the face is something rather like the basis of all relationships. The face is a force in and of itself: 'The sociological significance of the eye has special reference to the expression of the face as the first object of vision between man and man' (Simmel 1969: 359). He identifies the face as the 'geometric chart' through which the individual is able to approach an appreciation of the life, and emotions of the other as well as of 'the immutability of his being'. The face is 'the symbol of all that which the individual has brought with him as the pre-condition of his life' (Simmel 1969: 359). Simmel implies that the reciprocity of glances is a social fact which exists prior to any arrangement in institutions or laws. He implies that there are some human relationships which are outside of the boundaries of the milieu of the societal. Not dissimilar themes can be found in the work of Emmanuel Levinas, although whereas Simmel operates in terms of sociological narratives, Levinas operates in terms of the narratives of ethics. Moreover, whereas Simmel discusses the face in terms of an attempt to explain the basis of social and cultural relationships, Levinas discusses the face in terms of an attempt to explain the basis of ethical responsibility between the self and others.

Levinas believes that: 'The face is a fundamental event. Among the many modes of approach and diverse ways of relating to being, the action of the face is special' (Levinas 1988: 168). For Levinas the face 'is an irreducible means of access, and it is in ethical terms that it can be spoken of . . . the face . . . is a demand; a demand not a question' (Levinas 1988: 169). The demand is of the order that the individual has a responsibility towards the face of the other; a responsibility not to consign it to useless suffering, a responsibility not to refuse to recognize its frailty. But if the face makes this demand, Levinas knows too well that the face has no force to compel others to practise their responsibilities towards it. Although the face might be an ethical authority, 'one can do the opposite of what the face demands. The face is not a force. It is an authority. Authority is often without force' (Levinas 1988: 169).

As such, the question which Levinas inspires, and which Simmel can perhaps go some way towards answering, is precisely how and why it can be that the authority of the face might be denied to such an extent that it becomes possible to do the opposite of what the face demands. (Here it is not necessary to think only of major affronts to the demands of the face such as the Holocaust. It is possible to think of much smaller affronts such as the turning away of the glance from the face of a beggar in the street. We turn away our glance because gazing at poverty punctures reserve. Moreover, given that the glance might well be structured to some extent by social and cultural preconceptions, it is possible that the face of the other will not be apprehended as making demands upon me; to the contrary it might well be apprehended as proof that the impoverished other needs to pull him or her self out of their own misery. This latter reaction is bolstered and justified to a considerable degree by the economic accommodations to the culture of contentment.)

The answers which Simmel offers to this question of why and how the face which has authority lacks force are quite mundane but perhaps all the more pertinent for that. Firstly, Simmel implies the conclusion that in the city the face lacks force because it is apprehended through the sensual ensemble of looking and listening which is precisely assaulted by the city. The face of the other becomes one more thing about which the individual has few reasons to be anything other than utterly blasé. The face of the other lacks force because it is socially constructed and existentially experienced as not mattering terribly much. Moreover, Simmel is quite clear in his own mind that the reciprocity of glances upon eyes and faces 'can only be maintained by the shortest and straightest line between the eyes, and the smallest deviation from it, the slightest glance aside, completely destroys the unique character of this union' (Simmel 1969: 358). The point is that the city is full of things which can cause a deviation or distraction of glances; other people or traffic might get in the way, buildings might obstruct views, something dramatic might be happening on the other side of the street or beyond the window pane. Secondly, Simmel can lead to the conclusion that the face of the other lacks force because it is actually incompatible with the naturalized demands and requirements of the dialectic of reification. Here then, the face of the other does not have any force to compel a recognition of its ethical authority precisely because it is experienced as flying in the face of relationships and

99

arrangements which are confronted as if they are natural (and so social constructions once again become things about which nothing can be done. They allow for no alternative whilst the face becomes liable to experience as rather more contingent; about which something can indeed be done).

Simmel emphasizes the tendency of the face to lead to an appreciation of others purely on the basis of their being: 'To the extent to which we thus perceive the face of a person, there enters into social relations, in so far as it serves practical purposes, a super-practical element. It follows that a man is first known by his countenance, not by his acts' (Simmel 1969: 359). Simmel continues to point out that: 'The face as a medium of expression is entirely a theoretical organ; it does not act, as the hand, the foot, the whole body.' The face: 'transacts none of the internal or practical relations of the man, it only tells about him' (Simmel 1969: 359). That telling of the man through the face is a categorical telling of presence, of reciprocity and, taking Simmel in the direction of Levinas, of responsibility.

But if Hannah Arendt is correct to argue that the *vita activa* has been rearticulated so that man as *animal laborans* tends to be increasingly dominant then it is precisely the kind of theoretical knowledge of the individual which is implied by the face which is likely to be identified as least relevant for knowing what other humans are and what they mean. *Animal laborans* is a definition of what it is to be human which stresses the practical possibilities of the hand and the body over and above the purely categorical statements which are made by the face. *Animal laborans* means that the being which is registered by and signified in the face is likely to be accorded much less significance than the doing which is carried out by the hand. As Simmel saw it, the deepening of the division of labour and the tendency towards reification has as one of its consequences a situation in which: 'The individual has become a mere cog in an enormous organization of things and powers.' This organization which stands over and above any given individual: 'tears from his hands all progress, spirituality, and value in order to transform them from their subjective form into the form of a purely objective life' (Simmel 1950: 422). In these terms then, the authority of the face is exactly something which has to be overcome if *animal laborans* is to reign triumphant. At most, the face will be a signification of objectivity not subjectivity.

The *vita contemplativa* is able to do little or nothing about this problematic status of the face of the other. In so far as the *vita contemplativa* itself is concerned, quiet as either a social and cultural situation or an environmental experience is impossible. This is indeed an un-quiet world. The culture of contentment is crumbling at the edges as the state-funded support systems for the well-being of the relatively affluent are undermined by a lack of long-term policy or the simple lack of funding which is the other side of the lowering of taxation thresholds (to this extent then part of the economic accommodation to the culture of contentment might well have been seriously flawed). The holders of what were once believed to be jobs for life are being made redundant because computer systems are more efficient (and in principle less unpredictable) than human beings. The cities are so noisy and fast that the only possible escape and, seemingly, the only possible chance for existential survival is into oneself and, therefore, away from a concern with the others who are thus consigned to moral and human insubstantiality.

That escape into the self has to be a psychic and emotional process. It cannot be spatial because not even the domestic sphere can keep out an overwhelming influx of stimulants. Indeed, un-quiet is so much an element of second nature that it is impossible to think about its absence; impossible to think without it. Noise has become one of the main escape routes from the un-quiet which is produced on the city streets. When we get home we relax by playing loud music or by turning on the television. Quiet has in fact become something we do not like even when we can find it. Quiet oppresses too much. It is too empty and too demanding.

5

ESCAPING

Contemplation is an activity (of relative physical inactivity) which is predicated upon the occupation of specific and peculiarly social and cultural spaces and places. By extension then, the more general and systematized *vita contemplativa* (more general and systematized to the extent that the *vita contemplativa* is the socially organized and demarcated province of contemplation) stands as the expression of the entirely and self-consciously social and cultural existence. It is a life which is, according to its own requirements, quite divorced from anything which might possibly be construed as existing by nature. This foundation of the *vita contemplativa* has its roots in Aquinas and through to Arendt. Aquinas initiated the case subsequently made by Arendt of the identification of contemplation with experiential and environmental quiet standing apart from the un-quiet of the mundane relationships of the fabrication of objective things. That fabrication is a problem to the extent that it tends to become identified as the essential and natural activity of humanity and, furthermore, to the extent that the products of fabrication tend to become reifications.

Yet fabrication is the precondition of contemplation. The situations of contemplation have to be made. In other words, perhaps of all the things which are made in and through social and cultural relationships, the *vita contemplativa* is something like their crystallization. Perhaps more than anything else, fabrication makes it possible to think about fabrication. Fabrication produces the material freedoms which contemplation requires (not least the freedom from care about the satisfaction of the material demands and possibly even the urges of the body). It also produces the things in terms of which contemplation takes place. And it is exactly this debt to fabrication which makes contemplation so very vulnerable to tendencies towards reification.

All of this means that the *vita contemplativa* has to be, and always has to remain, a self-consciously social and cultural activity and practice. It is established in exclusively social and cultural contexts to such an extent that any hint that contemplation might take place as if by nature is quite oxymoronic. If it becomes interpreted or experienced as like an aspect of second nature, the *vita contemplativa* is threatened with attack if not, for that matter (and lapsing into catastrophism), terminal decay. It certainly becomes impossible to imagine as a critical engagement with the world or a 'No' saying. Contemplation and nature are qualities and situations which are necessarily constructed as polar opposites and mutually incompatible. But, within this narrative opposition, nature is seen as the dangerous intruder into places from which it should be excluded. Contemplation is the potential victim.

The *vita contemplativa* as Aquinas and subsequently Arendt established it is primarily threatened because the world is experientially and environmentally so noisy that there remain no situations of quiet. Here, it is not just the case that, following Huizinga, we are absolutely incapable of imagining how quiet the world used to be (Huizinga of course talks about the Middle Ages in Northern Europe, but technologically that world is largely identical to the world which shaped Aquinas's description of the preconditions of contemplation). It is not just the case that contemplation is impossible for us because its absolute precondition of absolute quiet has disappeared. After all, noise and quiet are not experiential absolutes. They are relative conditions and situations. It is unlikely that even the inhabitants of Huizinga's medieval towns considered themselves to be able to experience absolute quiet. In a much more boringly ordinary way, for us the world is noisy because of the cars and machines which have increased in volume within living memory. Indeed, that increase has occurred on a global canvas; it has taken place so quickly and over such a spatial spread that it virtually escapes experiential comprehension. The increase in the volume of machines has occurred as if it was obeying nothing other than a natural law.

The world is also noisy in a more metaphorical fashion. It is metaphorically noisy because of the preponderance of fleeting appearances. Appearances have the ability to move so quickly, and lines of vision can be interrupted so often by so many other lookers or by buildings or vehicles, that our eyes can only very rarely enjoy the quiet of resting on a single image. Moreover, and as Georg Simmel stressed, the confusions generated by what we see are attenuated by the profound lack of clarity of what we hear. Just as we see disappearing people and things, so we hear only the shouts above the engines. We rarely hear all there is to hear. The worlds we experience and inhabit are so noisy that we do not so much contemplate them as practice an emotional withdrawal.

Noise means that quiet disappears along with the possibility of contemplation. Noise transcends the boundaries which Aquinas took pains to establish between quiet and un-quiet. The monastery walls cannot keep out the noise from the streets which hum on the other side. Noise means that the situations of un-quiet can never be entirely ignored. Consequently then, the social and cultural terrain is flattened out. Everywhere is noisy; nowhere is quiet. Everyone practises emotional withdrawal; no one practises emotional engagement. Everyone experiences their situation and existence as the way it must be; no one experiences it as entirely social and cultural as opposed to natural.

From the point of view of Aquinas and Arendt this tendency is extremely problematic because it implies that all spaces and places tend to become experientially similar. That sense of similarity is born of the tendency of fabrication to become reification. And to the extent that anywhere tends to become like everywhere else it tends to become increasingly difficult to identify clear and allegedly definite zones of objectivity between the social and the cultural on the one hand and the natural on the other hand. Contemplation is thus threatened with collapse precisely because the homes of contemplation cannot be identified. Neither is it terribly easy to identify precisely what milieux or things contemplation might be about; after all it is hard to know where the social and cultural begin and where they end. All imaginative objects are thrown into a situation of generalized objectlessness. Such tendencies imply a decay of the preconditions of the *vita contemplativa* and, in so far as contemplation is experienced as less and less likely, so social and cultural self-consciousness is prone to diminish. In this situation of generalized second nature, the remnants of contemplation do not play on or exacerbate a specifically social and cultural milieu. Rather they are more likely to provide intellectual and ideational accommodations to the worlds individuals find themselves in. Contemplation becomes an activity of enchantment and contentment. It does not at all tend to be a challenge to the pretence that things are simply the way that things have to be.

That is the logic of the narrative I have been developing. But that narrative runs against a very obvious and major problem. By that narrative logic, this book could not be possible. On the one hand, I have been arguing that the *vita contemplativa* is decreasingly possible as social and cultural relationships become both exceedingly noisy and increasingly like nature. Yet on the other hand, I have developed that argument in the context of a speculative, and indeed contemplative, essay about the human condition in situations which are experienced in the finding not making (in the reification not the fabrication). I have contemplated the impossibility of contemplation. But it is possible to hold this paradox together if the *vita contemplativa* is reconstituted and placed on a different terrain than that which Aquinas and Arendt placed it. I want to propose that in the world which is experientially found not made, contemplation plays on the diametrically opposite terrain to that emphasized by Aquinas and Arendt.

Against Aquinas and Arendt I propose that in the noisy world the *vita contemplativa* can only be founded in a struggle to wrest un-quiet from the quiet of contentment and the acceptance of reification. Quiet has become too seductive and too easy to be able to do very much by way of offering even the barest hint that the human condition might be rescued from reification. For us in the noisy world which we experientially find not make, quiet is a way of escape from un-quiet. It is a refusal to make anything other than our own private defences against the confusions and stresses of existence in the cities. Quiet is quietude. As such, un-quiet becomes the source, place and avenue of engagement. Un-quiet becomes a way of engaging with the world. That un-quiet involves a refusal on the part of the individual or group to accept the conceit that she, he or it is receiving their just desserts. Morally it implies a refusal to accept that the others 'over there' have to remain beyond consciousness and beyond the orbit of responsibility. A sense of un-quiet becomes the basis of an ability to do something other than quietly accept the benefits one gains from the culture of contentment. A sense of un-quiet might be able to transcend situational quiet and the emotional withdrawal from the world which noise precipitates.

Contemplation consequently becomes possible to imagine and practise. It becomes a state of mind. What this means is that contemplation ceases to be necessarily associated with specific situations and experiences. Contrary to Aquinas, and more implicitly contrary to Arendt, when contemplation becomes a product of a state of mind it becomes, in principle at least, something which might be carried out by any group or individual. Contemplation is democratized and is no longer the exclusive province of groups which might well tend to identify themselves as some kind of elite. Moreover, even though contemplation is a state of mind rather more than it is a situational or experiential condition, it is not at all an activity which exists solely in the minds of men and women. It is not a property of some nebulous realm of ideas. It is important to stress that even when it is associated with a state of mind rather than monasteries of one description or another, contemplation remains as a specifically social and cultural activity with social and cultural preconditions of existence.

For the *vita contemplativa* of the found world, of the world which is experienced as reified rather more than it is experienced as fabricated, the preconditions of contemplation are somewhat different than they are conventionally assumed to be. In this situation, the foundations established by Aquinas, and taken more or less for granted by Hannah Arendt, have become aspects of that constituency of things which stand in need of questioning if a possibility of contemplation is to be forged out of the dull material of apparent nature. As such, distanciation as the precondition of the *vita contemplativa* tends to be replaced by the state of mind of alienation. In so far as this replacement does not occur, and in so far as the erstwhile agents of contemplation are incapable (through either the seduction of their own contentment or situational pressures) of experiencing a sense of alienation in relation to the circumstances which surround them, contemplation will indeed tend to be about little more than intellectual accommodation with the culture of contentment.

Since the *vita contemplativa* is about the making of a specifically human condition from the stuff of first or second nature, so it must contain a measure of critique (after all, any acceptance of this world as the best or the only world is precisely an acceptance of it as natural). And that critique, in its turn, requires a sense of alienation: 'In a sense, every critic is alienated from the society he criticizes, at odds with the complacency and self-satisfaction of (some of) his fellows' (Walzer 1989: 8). Here, alienation can be defined in a relatively straightforward way to refer to feelings of estrangement from a situation, group or, indeed, specific social and cultural relationships and arrangements. Such a feeling makes the banal seem fascinating. Like the alienation effect in Brechtian theatre, this state of mind of estrangement has the consequence for the individual of experientially setting the action of the world before her or him rather than allowing the individual easily to feel that she or he is involved directly in that action. As Brecht said: 'If empathy makes something ordinary of a special event, alienation makes something special of an ordinary one. The most hackneyed everyday incidents are stripped of their monotony when represented as quite special' (Brecht 1973: 368). (Of course, the developmental, if not indeed evolutionary, implications of Brecht's version of Marxism have absolutely no place in the account of alienation and contemplation I am trying to suggest.) Critique is precisely the means of that making something special out of what is otherwise all too ordinary and banal.

(Even though I have emphasized the experience and the existential situation of alienation, I hope it is clear from everything else that has been said in this book that I am not falling into the trap of using psychological categories to explain sociological situations. Alienation is not an internal psychic product even though it is a state of mind. The argument of this book is precisely that states of mind, existential experiences and social and cultural relationships and arrangements are all intimately related. It is through the experiences of situations and the extent to which those experiences can be naturalized – so that they can be interpreted as like categories and as like states of mind about which little or nothing can be done – that individuals construct and confront the world and thereby act in terms of it. States of mind are also fabrications which might tend to become reifications.)

The state of mind of alienation turns contemplation into a choice. And it has to be a choice if it is to avoid the fate of reification and establishment as second nature. But the choice is a hard one to make. The choice is difficult because the culture of contentment is so much easier and so much more comforting. It is quite hard to want to make one's own existence hard to bear when in fact it might be possible to experience it as extremely easy. Contemplation consequently requires a more or less voluntary decision by the individual (or the group; but the choice is much more likely to be an individual affair) to interpret the situations of the world she or he experiences as problems to be confronted. In turn this means that the decision to choose to practise contemplation is fundamentally moral. It is a choice which, however implicitly, involves a commitment to a rehumanization of the world and an attempt to deconstruct the material and intellectual shackles of reification.

The choice of contemplation is also difficult because it means that the individual who has so chosen can never again rest easily with the others she or he meets and enters into relationships with. For the individual who chooses the *vita contemplativa*, those others will be actual or potential sites of enquiry, while for the others the individual will be an actual or potential threat and affront to their contentment or sense of the inevitability of their existences. The *vita contemplativa* requires a wilful removal of the self from social and cultural conformity.

But the pressures towards conformity are quite considerable. This is yet another of the implications of the tendency towards reification and the establishment of second nature. Indeed, social and cultural relationships are liable to become, and to be experienced as, reifications which require a certain level of conformity on the part of individuals to the extent that they are subsumed within the category of society. As Hannah Arendt says: 'society expects from each of its members a certain kind of behavior, imposing innumerable and various rules, all of which tend to "normalize" its members, to make them behave, to exclude spontaneous action or outstanding achievement' (Arendt 1958: 37–38). Arendt justifies this claim on the grounds that, for her, society represents a situation in which rules and norms of behaviour are imposed equally upon all individuals regardless of their social and cultural status and group membership (in other words, and to put the matter into Weberian terminology, society is an ensemble of norms and arrangements which exist and operate without regard to persons). For Arendt: 'the realm of the social has finally, after several centuries of development, reached the point where it embraces and controls all members of a given community equally and with equal strength' (Arendt 1958: 38).

Moving out a little from Arendt, it is interesting to bring

together her identification of society as conformist and normalizing with Simmel's account of the perplexity of metropolitan life. Even though Arendt and Simmel are talking in somewhat different terms, it is nevertheless the case that both of them are also talking about the relationships, arrangements and experiences which emerge and arise when the individual enters into public spaces (and when the requirements of those public spaces enter into the minds of individuals). Conformity and perplexity therefore stand as the two poles between which it is likely that all relationships in and of public spaces are likely to be experienced and interpreted by the individual. (It must be stressed that what I am calling public spaces are not at all identical with Arendt's concept of the public realm. I am referring to concrete and material urban spaces whereas Arendt is referring to the polis of ancient political thought. Arendt talks about the public realm as part of her narrative of decline and fall; she identifies it as a legacy from the Greek city-states which allowed for individuality and difference but which has been conquered by the modern rise of society which is equalizing.)

In Arendt's account then, society means the imagination and the treatment of all individuals as identical and equal in all important respects: 'we see the body of peoples and political communities in the image of a family whose everyday affairs have to be taken care of by a gigantic, nation-wide administration of house-keeping' (Arendt 1958: 28). Consequently, society stands as an affront to what Arendt identifies as one of the basic foundations of the human condition; the plurality of human beings. For Arendt, it is precisely that plurality which creates the terrain and the requirement for individual and human action (Arendt 1958: 9–10), but in so far as society establishes a conceit of homogeneity it denies the possibility of action. There is no need for action because there are no differences which might constitute the terrain of that action. The interpretation of humans as acting beings is replaced with the interpretation of humans as behaving beings. Action becomes unnecessary if not, indeed, experientially impossible. Either we are all the same because we are all members of the same giant family of society or we are utterly different and beyond immediate concern because we are members of a different society.

In the giant administered family of society, all individuals are understood as much the same; as inclined towards the norm. For

Arendt this assumption is represented in the knowledges which are constituted on the terrain of society. According to her analysis these knowledges will tend to stress normative conditions, underemphasize the significance of spontaneous human action and, in all, reduce humanity to a homogeneous block. These tendencies are most clearly represented in the emergence of economics. According to Arendt, economics as a discipline rests on 'the assumption that men behave and do not act with respect to one another'. Economics established itself as a science to the extent that individuals (and humanity itself) could be understood not as a seething and contingent mass of actions but as a single whole of behaviours. Economics, 'could achieve a scientific character only when men had become social beings and unanimously followed certain patterns of behavior, so that those who did not keep the rules could be considered to be asocial or abnormal' (Arendt 1958: 39).

If, for Arendt, economics is the discipline of conformist and normalizing society then 'its chief technical tool' is statistics (Arendt 1958: 39). Despite its sophistication Arendt's account of the social and cultural implications of statistics is unfortunately somewhat less interesting than it might have been. She sees statistics monolithically as an attempt to reduce all relationships to the certainties of the laws of numbers. According to Arendt, statistics mean that the world is denuded of the human quality of action: 'acts or events can statistically appear only as deviations or fluctuations. The justification of statistics is that deeds and events are rare occurrences in everyday life and in history.' For Arendt, this conceit is offensive because: 'the meaningfulness of everyday relationships is disclosed not in everyday life but in rare deeds, just as the significance of a historical period shows itself only in the few events that illuminate it' (Arendt 1958: 39). This is too flat. Arendt is so concerned to rescue action and plurality from the behaviour and homogeneity generated by and for statistics that she tends to see statistics as an operation solely in the service of conformity.

In itself, Arendt's depiction of statistics is not inaccurate. But it is only half the picture. Perhaps Arendt has rather tended to take the proclamations of the social statisticians, who announce that they can find the laws which govern social and cultural relationships, too much at face value. The point is that even though statistics might well operate as if it can quantify and ultimately explain everything, the statistical enterprise is actually self-defeating. That tendency towards self-defeat is not, as Arendt would want to argue, due to the almost transcendental abilities of the unique action or event. It is due to the hunger of statistics to try to quantify and classify everything all the more accurately.

A more dialectical appreciation of the conceits and aporia of the statistical enterprise has been offered by Ian Hacking. Hacking contends that statistics emerged in the first decades of the nineteenth century as an attempt to control populations (and thus, to put this into Arendt's terms, to reduce the significance of spontaneous action by replacing it with an emphasis on regular behaviour). But he also contends that: 'Overt statistical study of populations comes to amass gigantic quantities of data that are seldom effective in controlling or altering the populations of study in the ways intended' (Hacking 1982: 280). Hacking's point is that, the conformist tendencies and inclinations of statistics notwithstanding, the enterprise actually subverts itself. Hacking explains that statistics emerged in order to control entire populations, but in so doing, statistics divided the population into subcategories. The entire population was more and more cut up into subunits until the population itself became little more than a statistical abstraction or an agglomeration of smaller groups and classes. In other words, as the concern with global knowledge and control deepens, so the classifications of the population become ever more complicated: 'Enumeration demands kinds of things or people to count. Counting is hungry for categories' (Hacking 1982: 280).

If a population is to be rendered conformist it must be interpreted as malleable. But one of the effects of the nineteenth-century concern with enumeration, 'was to create new categories into which people had to fall, and so to create and to render rigid new conceptualizations of the human being' (Hacking 1982: 281). Conformism only works if individuals and groups can be changed, but the increasing precision of statistical classification tied individuals and groups to ever more rigid and fixed identities. Furthermore, statistics subverts itself because, with the concern to establish the rules and norms of behaviour, it has to identify the foundations of disorder and normlessness. In the quest to find the laws of normality and order, statistics have to concentrate on everything which is perceived as precisely abnormal and disorderly. Statistics enhance the sense of the absence

111

of conformity. (For example, the contemporary measure of the orderliness of a society is usually the crime statistics; as such crime needs to be measured and forced into consciousness if order is to be known and made possible. But such a concentration on crime can only show that order is not a normative condition.) Statistics generate yet more of the very issues and situations which are identified as problems which need to be overcome (for a more general treatment of these kinds of processes of the social and cultural construction of ambivalence, see Bauman 1991).

Even though statistics might therefore be a very questionable way of establishing the ground of conformity and conformism, it is nevertheless the case that the emergence of statistical approaches to the understanding and the appreciation of social and cultural relationships does say important things about how the human condition is understood. Despite the shortcomings of her too monolithic account of the implication and basis of statistics, Arendt is right to contend that statistics, and what might well be called the statistical imagination, does indeed imply the replacement of action with behaviour as the key principle of the interpretation of relationships: 'society, on all its levels, excludes the possibility of action' (Arendt 1958: 37). Statistics also require that the possible answers to the question of what it means to be human will all tend to be reduced to the position of the individual in the system of classifications and, quite probably, the position of the individual in relation to some milieu of behaviour such as labour (Hacking 1982: 293). Furthermore, statistics also mean that law-like processes tend to come to dominate the interpretation of the world; the acts of human fabrication become less important than the erstwhile processes of which they are said to be a part: 'deeds will have less and less chance to stem the tide of behavior, and events will more and more lose their significance, that is, their capacity to illuminate historical time' (Arendt 1958: 40).

Statistics are one reflection of the tendency of the world we have made to become rather more like the world we simply find. But statistics also express the reification of the possibilities of the individual. The individual becomes a performer of a set role rather than a possible actor in a play which is written as it is produced. This situation not only means that contemplation becomes difficult because it stands out of line with everything which the statistical and behaviourist imagination establishes as necessary. This situation also means that, for all individuals, existence is likely to be experienced as something which is imposed upon them rather than as something which individuals choose for themselves.

In a world entirely dominated by the conformism and conformity of society and its technical arm of statistics, individual life would be more or less impossible. It would certainly be devoid of any sense of the possibility of individual or group production of existential meanings and truths. But of course, individual life is immensely possible, and individuals do tend to experience themselves as the subjective agents of their own wishes and desires. The pessimistic implications of the narrative of Arendt (and indeed myself) only casts light on one aspect of the experiential situation of the individual in the world. Even if individuals experience life and relationships in the public spaces of society as conformist and perplexing, they come to terms with those experiences of imposition and confusion by turning to what is taken to be the authenticity of the private personal sphere.

Arendt argues that the contemporary definition and understanding of the private sphere is radically different to that which was known to the Greeks and the Romans. For the Greeks, 'a life spent in the privacy of "one's own" . . . outside the world of the common, is "idiotic" by definition', while for the Romans, 'privacy offered but a temporary refuge from the business of the *res publica*' (Arendt 1958: 35). In other words, in ancient thought, the private sphere was synonymous with a situation of deprivation. For the Greeks the private sphere meant deprivation of the stimulation of relationships in common while for the Romans it meant deprivation of the duties and rights of the citizen: 'A man who lived only a private life . . . was not fully human' (Arendt 1958: 35). According to Arendt, we would hardly agree with either the Greeks or the Romans because for us the private sphere is held to be a milieu of authenticity in which it is possible for the individual to practise precisely her or his individuality and make existential truth.

The modern turn to the private was, according to Arendt, 'discovered as the opposite . . . of the social [sphere]' (Arendt 1958: 35). This opposition between the social and the private has two roots. Firstly, it is due to the tendency of society to become established as a huge administered family which will defend and nourish the life processes of the individual and the community alike after the immediate family has ceased to be materially or politically self-sufficient. As such, society took over functions which were previously the preserve of the family and, on the other side of this coin, the family became an aspect of the wider society. The boundary line which the Greeks and the Romans assumed between the political and the private is wholly blurred (to such an extent that we can say what the Greeks or the Romans could never have said; the personal is political). Secondly, the opposition is due to the tendency of society to reify the situation of the individual so that she or he is reduced to a statistical mean or a position in the division of labour. The private becomes the home of everything about the individual which cannot be subsumed within averages or labour.

The private sphere thus becomes a place outside of the functions of the normal or of production. It becomes a place of experiential consumption and, thus, of the inversion of the demands of relationships in the public places and spaces of society. The private sphere is the place where the individual can be what he wills to be rather than where he has to be what he is required to be. The private sphere is predominantly experienced as a last refuge of making not finding (for men at least in so far as they are socially and culturally constructed as the subjects who experience the confusions of public life most sharply; for women in so far as they are kept within reified gendered roles, it is likely that the relative evaluations of the social and the private spheres will be reversed). As Arendt says: 'the four walls of one's private property offer the only reliable hiding place from the common public world, not only from everything that goes on in it but also from its very publicity, from being seen and being heard'. Inside our homes we can become deep and authentic individuals. After all, 'A life spent entirely in public, in the presence of others, becomes, as we would say, shallow. While it retains its visibility, it loses the quality of rising into sight from some darker ground' (Arendt 1958: 63). Indeed, 'The only efficient way to guarantee the darkness of what needs to be hidden against the light of publicity is private property, a privately owned place to hide in' (Arendt 1958: 63). (This passage of course begs the question of the nature of privacy for individuals who cannot hide from the light of publicity; for individuals who own no property in either a material or a moral sense.)

The private sphere becomes identified as a place of escape and as a place which might permit the authentic playing out of the self in so far as it is experienced and interpreted as a place of quiet in relation to the situational and experiential un-quiet of the social relationships of the public places. (And again the problem of the lack of a place to hide reappears. Is it the case that individuals who cannot hide from publicity will never be accorded the status of a true and authentic identity by those who can so hide, and who are very content about their ability so to do? If debates about beggars on the streets of Britain are to be believed, this is a distinct possibility – especially if such a denial of the humanity of the beggar might win political plaudits.)

If society means conformity and the sense of a tension between truth to self and truth to others (if it thus means a kind of un-quiet), the private sphere consequently means authenticity (it thus means a kind of quiet). But it is a quiet which has to be made. That making consists in a turn to intimacy. Intimate private relationships become the point of escape from the un-quiet and the experiential inauthenticity of relationships in public. Intimacy becomes the site of all hopes and ambitions for the practice, revelation and demonstration of the true self when society and urban spaces are confronted as overbearingly normalizing or confusing. Arendt goes so far as to draw a direct causal linkage between forms of cultural production and the importance of intimacy as an escape from the constraints of society. According to Arendt, the 'flowering of poetry and music from the middle of the eighteenth century until almost the last third of the nineteenth' along with 'the rise of the novel, the only entirely social art form, coinciding with a no less striking decline of all the more public arts, especially architecture' can be taken to stand as 'testimony to a close relationship between the social and the intimate' (Arendt 1958: 36).

Arendt offers a suspiciously neat and tidy account of how the rise of society has led to a turn to intimacy. She explains that intimacy becomes increasingly important as society dominates the public sphere and, in turn, as the private sphere is dissolved. In these terms then, intimacy is so important because it is all that remains after all the firm spheres of the human condition which were established in ancient thought and activity have been caused to wither away. Intimacy is the only thing about which we can any longer be certain. For Arendt, 'the modern discovery of intimacy seems a flight from the whole outer world into the inner subjectivity of the individual, which formerly had been sheltered and protected by the private realm' (Arendt 1958: 61). Which formerly had been protected . . .

According to Arendt, the private realm has lost its solidity and security because the private property which formerly lent it an objectivity has been transformed. Whereas property was once the possession of a family over time or connected with definite situations and places, now it is the possession of a single individual who is invested with the right to dispose of it more or less as she or he pleases. Private property has ceased to be immobile (and objective) and has, instead, become mobile (and objectless). For Arendt, private property has become wealth and it has, consequently, 'lost its private use value which was determined by its location'. It has instead 'acquired an exclusively social value . . . determined through its ever-changing exchangeability whose fluctuation could itself be fixed only temporarily by relating it to the common denominator of money' (Arendt 1958: 61).

What all of this means is that, for Arendt, private property ceases to be a part of the world of fabrications (and of the fabricated world). Instead it becomes one contingent aspect of the individual (Arendt 1958: 62). (Arendt's point can be extended; as the value of property is fixed by money so it becomes commodified and liable to the processes of fetishization.) As such, private property and therefore the private sphere cannot at all operate or be established as anything like a home for humanity in the world. It is far too transient and uncertain for that. Arendt bewails, 'the abolition of private property in the sense of a tangible, worldly place of one's own' (Arendt 1958: 62). Intimacy emerges as the place and basis of home when all the other possible homes of the individual and humanity have been demolished. Intimacy is the emotion which is supposed to fill the void opened up by the tendency towards an objectless private sphere, a blurred public sphere and an overwhelming and an overbearing societal sphere. But for all of these things, 'the intimate is not a very reliable substitute' (Arendt 1958: 62).

The analysis and discussion of intimacy has been pushed to new lengths, and in new directions, by Anthony Giddens. Intimacy is defined by Giddens as something which 'should not be understood as an interactional description, but as a cluster of prerogatives and responsibilities that define agendas of practical activity' (Giddens 1993: 310). Intimacy is about rights and obligations, rights and obligations which are mutually respected and mutually practised. According to Giddens, a considerable part of the appeal of intimacy is due to the way it 'means the promise of democracy' in personal relationships. Indeed this promise is such that: 'We can envisage the development of an ethical framework for a democratic personal order, which in sexual relationships and other personal domains conform to a model of confluent love' (Giddens 1993: 309).

Giddens is suggesting that whatever wider and more general social and cultural arrangements might involve and require of individuals, the personal sphere is one of voluntary mutual relationships which are predicated upon a fundamentally democratic notion and practice of love. Giddens understands democracy to mean, 'discussion. . . . The conduct of open discussion is itself a means of democratic education: participation in debate with others can lead to the emergence of a more enlightened citizenry' (Giddens 1993: 307). If all of that sounds too much like political theory, then Giddens acknowledges that debt (Giddens 1993: 306) but he is perfectly happy to apply these criteria of a democratic polity to a study and description of the stakes of intimacy. Intimacy too is about discussion between partners so that individuals can know both others and themselves better than they previously did and otherwise might.

This knowledge requires respect and the practice of a principle of autonomy. Just as the democratic polity can only operate to the extent that it assumes a plurality of participants all of whom are autonomous from others, so intimacy has a similar foundation. According to Giddens: 'In the arena of personal life, autonomy means the successful realization of the reflexive project of self – the condition of relating to others in an egalitarian way. . . . Thus conceived, self-autonomy permits that respect for others' capabilities which is intrinsic to a democratic order' (Giddens 1993: 309). The principle of autonomy serves to make intimate relationships tend towards an absence of abusive power relationships and it also allows the individual space and a will to learn more about him or herself. It is in terms of this argument that Giddens stresses the rise and importance of self-directed practices and forms of knowledge such as therapy. After all, 'Therapy is not simply a means of coping with novel anxieties, but an expression of the reflexivity of the self.' This reflexivity of the self, this self-reflexivity, is 'a phenomenon which, on the level of the individual . . . balances opportunity and potential catastrophe in equal measure' (Giddens 1993: 305). Therapy stands as an example of how the individual becomes enlightened about self and, in so doing, how the individual learns to be an authentic self.

For Giddens, love is the emotional content of the personal sphere and, precisely because of this emphasis on love, the sphere is one of reciprocity, individual sovereignty and a committed subjectivity. In intimate relationships individuals are identified as freely acting subjects with their own intentions, wills and desires which the other partner respects. Giddens admits that this portrayal of a democratic intimacy might sound somewhat utopian but nevertheless: 'The changes that have helped transform personal environments of action are already well advanced, and they tend towards the realization of democratic qualities' (Giddens 1993: 309). He also claims that: 'A democratisation of the private sphere is today not only on the agenda, but is an implicit quality of all personal life that comes under the aegis of the pure relationship' (Giddens 1993: 305).

The pure relationship takes central place in Giddens's account of intimacy and the road to authenticity. The pure relationship is understood by him to be a means by which individuals 'determine the conditions of their own association' (Giddens 1993: 310). In other words, a pure relationship is one which individuals enter into and construct for themselves on the basis of their reflexive knowledge of self and other. The pure relationship is pure because it is made up as it goes along by individuals who desire to be authentic to themselves and respectful of the autonomy of the other. Giddens contends that: 'All relationships which approximate to the pure form maintain an implicit "rolling contract" to which appeal may be made by either partner when situations arise felt to be unfair or oppressive.' Giddens goes on in a way which emphasizes yet again the narrative and normative connection he wants to make between democratic political and personal arrangements: 'The rolling contract is a constitutional device which underlies, but is also open to negotiation through, open discussion by partners about the nature of the pure relationship' (Giddens 1993: 312). Indeed, and so democratically, so pluralistically: 'The imperative of free and open communication is the *sine qua non* of the pure relationship; the relationship is its own form' (Giddens 1993: 313).

What is interesting about all of this is how Giddens continually stresses the status of intimacy (codified in and as the pure

118

relationship) as a making of the world of the personal. He also continually stresses how that making of relationships with others leads to, if not indeed actively requires, an ongoing reflexive project of the making of the self. All of this making is motivated by a logic of a democratic principle of autonomy which implies that individuals are able to become all the more enlightened about what it is that they do (and do in their relationships with others). To this extent then it is not unreasonable to suggest that, if Giddens provides a plausible interpretation of the stakes and the appeal of intimacy, then an emotion like love can be one way in which the world can be experientially rescued for humanity and human being even though its societal arrangements might be tending towards almost absolute reification. Giddens perhaps shows how it is possible for individuals to continue to be human even as the world which surrounds them becomes second nature.

But there is a very major problem with Giddens's account. Giddens's account is based on a relatively straightforward conception of the personal realm. The realm revolves around what the individual does in intimate relationships and, qualitatively, it seems to imply some access to, or correspondence with, experiences of personal authenticity. It is noticeable that when Giddens talks about intimacy his awareness of wider social and cultural processes, institutions and relationships, tends to be pushed to one side. What Giddens forgets is the status of the personal sphere as, in fact, a social and cultural construct. Giddens seems to forget the point made by Hannah Arendt that individuals do not live in a world which is structured around a more or less clear divide between public and private milieux. Rather individuals live and experience a world which is established as society; as a milieu in which the dividing line between personal and public is always blurred. Because of the way he draws a narrative opposition, Giddens is unable to acknowledge 'the extraordinary difficulty with which we . . . understand the decisive division between the public and private realms, between the sphere of the polis and the sphere of household and family' (Arendt 1958: 27–28).

Giddens does not notice that the case he makes for intimacy and authenticity is also a case for a lack of intimacy and a treatment of the other in terms of a means–ends rationality which denies the status of the other as an autonomous subject. This kind of problem becomes quite clear when Giddens attempts to sketch a little of the detail of the supposed 'rolling contract' of the pure relationship. Giddens wants to show how the pure relationship can be established on a basis of mutual respect and how that mutuality can be negotiated and renegotiated to the benefit of the partners. What he shows instead is quite how personal relationships become a domain of potential inauthenticity if they are turned into contexts of self-reflexivity.

Giddens discusses a set of rules for a satisfying heterosexual relationship. He takes the rules from an advice book for women. The rules include such clauses as that which establishes that 'When my feelings are hurt, I'll tell my partner how I'm feeling rather than pouting, getting even, pretending I don't care or acting like a little girl' (Giddens 1993: 312). Now according to Giddens rules like these, 'however unsophisticated they might seem, if successfully applied help prise the individual's actions away from an unconsciously organised power game. In principle, they serve to generate increased autonomy at the same time as they demand respect from the other' (Giddens 1993: 313). But the rules can only achieve all of this at the possible expense of authenticity. The inauthenticity arises because, firstly, the supposedly personal relationship is being put into a broader social and cultural setting (of negotiation, of contract of reciprocity; of presentations of self rather than necessarily expressions of self) and, secondly, the individual is meant to alter her actions in order to bolster the heterosexual relationship. But it is not at all impossible to imagine situations in which authenticity to self means that the woman who devised the rules actually feels driven to 'act like a little girl'. It is perfectly possible that all the woman's reflexive negotiations of self have led her to the self-awareness that, in this specific situation, petulance is actually an extremely plausible and reasonable attitude to adopt. Giddens's faith in the pure relationship contains the problem that it is possible either that it means a constraint on self-reflexivity or that the relationship can only be maintained if the individuals subsume their experientially authentic feelings.

But his faith has other problems as well. Firstly, Giddens seems to be quite unaware of the possibility that most intimate relationships are not based on explicit contractarian negotiation and a deep self-knowledge which has emerged out of such practices as entry into therapy. It can be postulated that with his depiction of the pure relationship, and with his tendency to universalize it, Giddens is illicitly extrapolating very specific social and cultural attitudes. One wonders if any relationship anywhere is actually anything at all like a Giddensian pure relationship (and if any relationship anywhere can ever be like that). This problem is exacerbated because Giddens makes it plain that 'democracy implies that individuals have sufficient resources to participate in an autonomous way in the democratic process'. He says that the same precept 'applies in the domain of the pure relationship' (Giddens 1993: 314). Unfortunately, however, material resources are not equally distributed and neither do all individuals (or for that matter all social and cultural groups) have adequate access to enough resources to enable them to operate on a basis of autonomy. Giddens is presuming membership of the culture of contentment and utterly forgetting about the vast swathes of individuals and groups who experience material in-security. Perhaps he is even guilty of producing the sociological accommodation to the culture of contentment.

Secondly, and perhaps more worryingly, Giddens's whole argument seems to be based on a sleight of hand. He takes what he thinks ought to be the case in intimate relationships and uses that ideal to say what is the case. Not to put too fine a point on the matter, Giddens slips from the role of interpreter into the role of adviser. For example, at one point he discusses adult–child pure relationships. He asks whether an adult–child relationship can be democratic. He answers himself: 'It can, and should be, in exactly the same sense as is true of a democratic political order. It is a right of the child, in other words, to be treated as a putative equal of the adult' (Giddens 1993: 311). There can be absolutely no sociological justification for this assertion. It can only be justified on ethical grounds and yet a pure relationship 'does not deal in ethical absolutes' (Giddens 1993: 313). As such, either Giddens's claims about what ought to be are quite without justification or the concept of the pure relationship is plain wrong.

Even more than all of this, Giddens's account of intimacy can be objected to on the basis that, despite appearances, it does not allow for humanity in the face of reification. Giddens's work can be objected to on the grounds that it stands as little more than an acceptance of the reduction of humanity and human being to the status of *animal laborans*. The point is that with its denial of ethical absolutes and its emphasis on self-reflexive negotiation, Giddens's account of intimacy emphasizes doing over being. This emphasis is quite clear when Giddens makes statements of the order that: 'In relationships as elsewhere, obligations have to be treated as revisable in the light of negotiations carried on within them' (Giddens 1993: 311). Once again then, Giddens's position is one which makes it very hard to know how intimacy can have any kind of necessary connection with experiential authenticity. Such an interpretation and understanding of intimacy reduces the meaning of humanity to behaviour. Humanity becomes devoid of any qualities and capacities other than its ability to conform with the standards established within the norms and order of society. In the last instance and despite what are undoubtedly his own intentions, Giddens turns intimacy into yet another situation which is able to 'reduce man as a whole, in all his activities, to the level of a conditioned and behaving animal' (Arendt 1958: 41). These are some of the wider, and less pleasant, meanings of negotiation and compromise.

Giddens's account and interpretation of intimacy only really goes to illustrate Arendt's point about quite how unreliable intimacy is as a way of constructing an authentic individuality. On the one hand it is possible to suggest that intimacy, and a flight into a personal milieu, becomes all the more attractive as the world is experienced in terms of situations of un-quiet. Intimacy promises a realm of authenticity and of eye-to-eye contact which can thus be something of a balm to the wounds and perplexities of urban existence. On the other hand, if intimacy is constructed as a realm of authenticity and importantly as a situation of the knowing of authenticity, then it ironically leads to experiences of un-quiet. If intimacy is established on anything approaching an explicitly democratic basis then it is also made social and a perpetual problem to be negotiated away. I would suggest that it is precisely this problem which Giddens reveals. I would want to suggest that instead of offering a sociology of intimacy what Giddens actually provides is a plea for intimacy which shows immensely clearly why a flight into personal relationships is doomed to fail. As soon as intimacy is identified as a situation of the making of authenticity and of personal humanity, then it is turned into an unresolvable difficulty. Intimacy can only offer even the merest hint of a solution to the problems of un-quiet if it is understood to be always and possibly even necessarily pre-reflexive. In this vein, in this attempt to construct a refuge from un-quiet, intimacy takes the pre-reflexive form of love.

A fine instance of the seductive potential of a belief in the pre-reflexivity of love can be found in Roland Barthes's *A Lover's Discourse*. What is interesting about Barthes is how he tries to write about love even though the precise meaning of love always slips out of his grasp. This perpetual movement away from complete understanding is a product of the social and cultural construction of love as something which can never really be understood. It is that air of the impossibility of definite understanding which makes love experientially appear as pre-reflexive. Love can operate as a principle of quiet all the time it is never entirely captured in words; all the time it is a process without end.

Barthes shows how love can turn the individual into a subject who is experientially able to write her or his own existence as an an adventure (as an exercise of the making) rather than as a destiny imposed from outside, as if by nature (as an exercise of the finding). According to Barthes, the adventure of love has three stages. First comes the capture, when the individual is 'ravished by an image'. Second comes a series of encounters 'during which I ecstatically "explore" the perfection of the loved being . . . this is the sweetness of the beginning, the interval proper to the idyll' (Barthes 1983: 441). Third comes the period which retrospectively invests the second stage of exploration with the aura of a certain happiness: 'the sequel is the long train of sufferings, wounds, anxieties, distresses, resentments, despairs, embarrassments' (Barthes 1983: 441). Barthes claims that this love story in three stages is understood by the individual as having followed a trajectory which is not amenable to investigation: 'later on, in memory, the subject will telescope into one the three moments of the amorous trajectory; he will speak of "love's dazzling tunnel"' (Barthes 1983: 441–442). (The subject of whom Barthes speaks is almost certainly Roland Barthes himself.)

But this quiet is obtained at great expense. Even as love seems to make the individual all the more human so it actually makes the world all the less human. Love is precisely objectless in and of itself (it is impossible to point to it and say 'there is love'. It only becomes objective to the extent that it fastens onto another individual who is thus a means to the externalization of an emotion and not necessarily an end in him or her self). Consequently the pre-reflexivity of love appears to be natural. It blurs the distinction between the human and the natural milieux. Love is identified as able to make us more human even though it is said to strike us from outside. Love itself is somewhat inhuman. And that is why it is so attractive; that is why so many individuals are so seduced by it.

Love might stand as a chance of making quiet in an otherwise un-quiet world. But that chance can only succeed if the individual enters into a situation of bad faith and accepts as natural an emotion which is, in fact, a social and cultural construction. (After all, romantic love is not a universal property of social and cultural relationships.) Yet even that bad faith can be punctured. Whatever intellectual and emotional moves might be performed, love has a measure of un-quiet built into it. Love is not just an emotion; it is also the implication of bodily practices. Love is experientially social and cultural and natural at one and the same time. (This comment is made in full knowledge of the work of Foucault; his point is precisely that even though the bodily practices of love are not natural they are experienced by individuals as having that non-social and non-cultural status; Foucault 1979.)

Bryan Turner has stressed the importance of the realization that: 'For the individual and the group, the body is simultaneously an environment (part of nature) and a medium of the self (part of culture)' (Turner 1984: 38–39). Now if the phrase 'I love you' can be taken to represent love as a medium of the authentic self, then the physical, bodily attitudes of love can be taken to represent the environment of love. As love is embodied (and love is indeed and invariably embodied; it is an attitude of the body and involves bodily practices), it is tied to the accidents associated with the environment of the body. To a very crucial extent, love becomes dependent on contingencies of physical appearance. My love is not just what I will it to be. It is also likely to be dependent to a not inconsiderable extent on the attractiveness of my body to the person I would love. Consequently, my love, my chance of experiential quiet and refuge from confusion, is dependent on a body which might actually strike down my ambitions.

The tense relationship between love and the body was known by Pascal. As Pascal asked: 'But does he who loves someone on account of beauty really love that person? No; for the small-pox, which will kill beauty without killing the person, will cause him to love her no more' (Pascal 1931: 90). For Pascal, the attributes of physical beauty amount to 'borrowed qualities'. The bodily qualities say little or nothing about the individual as a human being and yet it is significantly in terms of those qualities that the definition of the individual by others is likely to be constructed. We do not choose our bodies but, Pascal is speculating, in a fundamental way it is through our bodies that others might well choose us. Much the same dilemma is raised by Pascal when he contemplates the length of Cleopatra's nose: 'had it been shorter, the whole aspect of the world would have been altered' (Pascal 1931: 48). Pascal's rather throwaway comment about Cleopatra's nose can be read as an instance of the complete confusion which can arise when it is impossible to say where the specifically social and cultural world begins and ends. The problem of the length of Cleopatra's nose is also a problem about how it might be possible to understand the status and the meaning of human being when it is influenced by natural forces.

When love is associated with bodily practices as opposed to bodily attractiveness then it is identified with the supposedly absolute authenticity and absolute reciprocity of sexual 'making love' (here then I am not at all talking about pornography and other practices which entirely reduce the other to the status of passive physical object). Sex is experientially identified as the *sine qua non* of pre-reflexivity; as the ultimate refuge. Sexual activity is open to identification as such a definite answer to perplexity and un-quiet because it is experienced as either natural or private or a personal affair about which the individual can become some kind of an expert. But it is exactly this possibility of expertise which makes sexual activity a source of un-quiet as well. It means that sexual activity (as and when it is involved in the making of love) might also cease to be an expression of anything approaching personal authenticity. It might well be little more than trick which has been learnt.

If for the moment Giddens's claim about the rolling contract of the pure relationship is accepted (and I am inclined to accept it purely for the sake of argument), then it is not improbable that sexual expertise might well be or become a clause in the contract. It is not impossible that the contract between the partners might embody a right and an obligation to the performance of a satis-fying sexual life. And so, once again, authenticity in personal relationships elevates situations of the doing over situations of the being; self-reflexivity possibly leads to a denial of what the self would rather do. The body, and specifically the embodiment of the emotion of love, might well be a source and opportunity of pleasure but that it can be a basis for the quiet of complete confidence and the complete absence of confusion, the basis of a wholly relaxed experience of self and subjectivity, is very unlikely.

The body is a problem because it is an environment of first nature which can never, ever, be kept out of social and cultural relationships (the attitude of the mortification of the flesh which Aquinas emphasized notwithstanding). Meanwhile, love offers only an inhuman refuge from the reification of fabrication because it only operates successfully if it is itself attributed with the status of existing as if by nature. Love is an escape from reification which is precisely a reification. And so it might not be much of a refuge at all. But without it life might well be experienced as immensely difficult to bear.

6

ENDING

At the beginning of this book we visited Martin Heidegger. He was looking at photographs of the earth and trying to understand what they portended. The image of the confused and worried Heidegger has run through this book. I have used the image as a way of teasing out some of the debates, and the implications of the debates, about what it means to be human in this world. I have been trying to develop an interpretation of our human condition; of the relationships and experiences of our being in the world. I have also been talking around the rather thorny problem of whether it is actually viable to uphold some notion of the human condition. For me the main problem is that there seem to be few persuasive sociological reasons to uphold a concept of the human condition, yet without it critical and moral discourses seem to become immensely tenuous. Without some almost transcendental concept of humanity and its condition, contemplation cannot possibly go very far beyond a simple registration and repetition of the arrangements of the everyday. But it is precisely that transcendental subject which seems to be quite improbable. Equally, even though it might not be the case that we all share Heidegger's concerns in the face of the photographs (for some people, photographs of the earth are quite beautiful and not at all disturbing; for other people the photographs are so familiar that they mean next to nothing), I think it is reasonable to suggest that Heidegger's concerns cut to the quick of who we are, who we might be, who we might be able to want to be.

The problem of being human (and of human being) emerges because the photographs imply the entry of the category of the human into a situation of ontological ambivalence. Experientially, the answer to the question of what it means to be human is also made less than entirely obvious. The story told in this book has to a considerable extent has been one of how a recognition of that ambivalence is socially and culturally avoided. After all, the kinds of worries which Heidegger expressed do not confront most individuals most of the time (or even a little of the time for that matter). On the one hand, Heidegger is confronting problems which are common to all of us and yet, on the other hand, what Heidegger talks about seems to be of little or no immediate relevance to what most other people tend to worry about. In these terms, Heidegger looking at the photographs and getting upset can be seen as an image of the kind of alienation which a critical contemplation of the world requires and re-produces. Heidegger is not just alienated from the earth and from the world, he is also alienated from his fellow human beings and, indeed, from any contented acceptance of who and what he might be. In this instance then, Heidegger can be taken to represent our conscience.

An appreciation of this combination of critical opportunity with what amounts to an existential curse has been developed by Stefan Morawski. Morawski has commented that for most of the time, in most relationships, individuals are 'harboured in famil-iarity with our past and actual surroundings, accustomed to our unshaken at-homeness in the world' (Morawski 1994: 181). But that at-homeness is liable to collapse at certain moments of anxiety and confusion. Morawski points to personal moments: 'when, for instance, we face our dearest's death or are threatened by hopeless illness or meet with great misfortunes or find no more sense in our professional activity' (Morawski 1994: 181). The list of anxieties which Morawski provides is, perhaps, too much centred on the experiences of the individual who is some-what decontextualized and removed from broader social and cultural situations of existence and experience. But what is interesting about the list is that it can be read as a catalogue of moves from quiet into un-quiet. The collapse of self-evidence and the alienation of the individual from everything which she or he has learned to take for granted produces anxiety and confusion but, also, the possibility of a critical engagement with the world.

To a considerable extent what Morawski is talking about is the existential implications for the individual of the collapse of the little worlds and situations of contentment which we all struggle to build in order to make ourselves feel at home in the world, in order to make the world make sense to us even though it might be noisy and fast, overbearing and overwhelming. Morawski continues to state what happens when what he calls 'at-homeness' is threatened: 'Then the world with the persons, things, events which were like the air we breathe yields to an assemblage of alien givens and, what is more, we change into beings strange to ourselves' (Morawski 1994: 181).

The situation Morawski is talking about has at its heart a problematization of the possibility that the individual might be able to experience him or her self as the sovereign centre of a world of his or her own making. The sense of certainty which might be connected with the writing of existence as a biographical adventure with a beginning, a middle and an end which is yet to come is rendered more or less difficult. The single and noble linear narrative fractures into a series of episodes which might or might not be continuous one with each other (a state of mind or experience of existence which itself is not too far removed from how, according to Simmel, the metropolis impacts upon the 'mental life' of its citizens).

It is very tempting to connect this situation described by Morawski with that which Peter Berger, Brigitte Berger and Hansfried Kellner have called the homeless mind (Berger, Berger and Kellner 1974). According to the Bergers and Kellner a sense of homelessness emerges when individuals experience their exis-tences as being lived under a plurality of signs and organizing principles. Homelessness emerges when we no longer know for sure who, where or why we are in the world (or, in Morawski's terms, when we no longer enjoy the sense of at-homeness). The most obvious major difference between Morawski and the Bergers and Kellner is that whereas the former, at least in the list I have already quoted, reduces the loss of at-homeness to per-sonal biographical events, the latter tend more to relate it to social and cultural processes, arrangements and relationships. For the Bergers and Kellner: 'The pluralistic structures of modern society have made the life of more and more individuals migratory, ever changing, mobile. In everyday life the modern individual con-tinuously alternates between highly discrepant and often contradictory social contexts.' Indeed: 'Not only are an increasing number of individuals in a modern society uprooted from their original social milieu [in Heidegger's terms of course, this uprooting might well be universal – or at least universal for everyone who has gazed at photographs from space], but, in addition, no succeeding milieu succeeds in becoming truly "home" either' (Berger, Berger and Kellner 1974: 165).

Within this analytic of homelessness there can only be one response to the shattering of the possibility of feeling oneself to be at home: a yearning for home (this conclusion is largely inevitable given the narrative precondition of homelessness). According to the Bergers and Kellner the experience of homelessness has, 'engendered its own nostalgias – nostalgias, that is, for a condition of "being at home" in society, with oneself and, ultimately, in the universe' (Berger, Berger and Kellner 1974: 77). For the Bergers and Kellner the experience of homelessness is likely to be so traumatic and disturbing that individuals will do virtually anything to avoid having to confront its stark presence. One of the avoidance strategies involves a steeling of oneself for the trials of the future (and for that matter of the present) through a return to the fondly remembered personal or societal homes of the past. That is tantamount to a return to contentment and, therefore, to a retreat into second nature.

Even though it might possess a high level of immediacy, I am not sure that the metaphor of homelessness, with its narrative corollary of a nostalgic search for home, is actually a fully rounded account of the existential implications of alienation. Of course, alienation can lead to a search for home. There is no basis upon which that claim can be doubted. But there is good reason to doubt whether any search for home, of either a nostalgic or futuristic vein (and the Bergers and Kellner place a great deal of hope in the promise of a socialist future; and therefore in the future of socialism – but aspects of that future have failed or been murdered). After all, a home is a fabrication which can tend to become a reification. It is not at all impossible that home will in its turn eventually produce the kinds of tensions and anxieties which generate and underpin the experience of existence as dominated by a plurality of possibly incommensurable principles (not least there will be an emergent plurality along the line of division between experiences of at-homeness and experiences of not-at-homeness). Neither is there any reason to believe that there is a homogeneous universal response to homelessness. Certainly some groups and individuals might respond to the experience of homelessness by a faith in home (a nostalgic home which will be found, a future home which will be built in order to be found by the children of the builders). But it is just as likely that the collapse of at-homeness is met with the experiential and existential response not of homelessness but of homesickness.

The metaphor of homesickness has the advantage over the metaphor of homelessness that it is much more dialectical. Whereas homelessness implies a trajectory from one situation to another, homesickness implies the potential simultaneity, or at the very least the potential oscillation of experience, between two somewhat different situations. On the one hand homesickness suggests a search for home. It suggests the seeking for a place of quiet and refuge from the noisiness and strains of relationships in and of the public. To this extent homesickness suggests the hope that Aquinas might retain some validity in the reified world of second nature. But homesickness also suggests a sickness if home is found. Homesickness is also the fear of finding a home which can be quiet, a home which requires a complete withdrawal from the generality of other individuals if it is to be maintained as a refuge. To this extent then homesickness implies the actual or potential experience of the quiet of home as rather more like a prison cell of solitary confinement than a place of repose in which the pieces of shattered individuality might be reassembled.

Homesickness is the search for home and the fear of not knowing how to live within its boring safety as soon as it is found. In so far as she or he experiences a certain homesickness, the individual is placed within a dialectical tension which is quite inescapable. The benefit of this situation is the possibility of the establishment of a critical distance between the individual and any pre-given social and cultural arrangements (and, as such, a critical reflection upon the world becomes possible). The cost of this situation is that the existential burden of this critical distance becomes a burden to be borne because it can never be thrown off in good faith. It can only be thrown off through a retreat into the belief that there is a least one thing, at least one aspect of life, which will remain once all of the expressions and representations of homesickness have been bracketed away. It can only be thrown off if it is presumed that there is some quality of existence which is transcendental, prior to and greater than the exigencies and difficulties of the here and now.

One aspect of that presumed realm of the transcendent is love. Love is a principle by means of which individual biographies can be written as a single narrative, by which the experience of existence can be interpreted as a journey towards quiet. Love is a principle which can reconcile the difficulties of homesickness precisely because it is constructed as so magical. The basis of that sense of magic is the social and cultural construction of love as a quality of relationships which has a force quite independently of the demands of institutions and arrangements (in other words, love stands as something rather like a counter-nature; it is experienced as like a natural force which makes demands that are much more powerful than those which are taken to be natural in mundane social and cultural relationships; it is a more natural kind of nature). Love is experienced as like magic because it is experienced as a 'boundless giving of oneself [which] is as radical as possible in its opposition to all functionality, rationality, and generality' (Weber 1948: 347). In these terms, love can be understood as the emotional counterpart to the tendencies towards the fetishization of commodities which exist long after they have become obsolete. These commodities also stand quite independently of any functionality.

What all of these forms of magic have in common, irrespective of their considerable ontological differences, is the aura of the mystification of the world and human being in it. What they have in common is the implication of an enchantment of the world which enables the individual to make some kind of sense of the world even as she or he experiences personal existence as fractured and possibly problematic. Love, like commodity fetishism, makes the world seem credible for the individual who would otherwise be all too liable to experience personal existence as immensely incredible.

Ironically then, the human condition in the fabricated-turned-reified world only makes sense for the individual to the extent that it is allowed to possess some inhuman qualities. It is only through this resort to the traces of enchantment that individuals can possibly come to terms with the ultimate contingency of everything they do and are, everywhere they are, all that they believe to be completely self-evident. It is only through a resort to the bad faith of love and other forms of enchantment that the human condition is endurable. Or, put another way, the human condition is inhabitable by humans only in so far as it is itself open to being experienced as quite inhuman. We can only endure the world we have made if we can allow ourselves to believe that actually we did not make it at all.

This situation not only means that the world is almost required to become like second nature if it is to be able to make sense, it also means that the world ceases to be something with which human action can engage. This is one of the most important reasons why such a situation can be called inhuman. It is inhuman not just because it is experienced as enchanted and magical; it is inhuman also because it cannot possibly allow for any of the action through which humanity plays on the terrain of the plurality of human beings and, in so doing, distinguishes itself from its surrounding environment as the simultaneous subject and object of enquiry, responsibility and commitment.

According to Hannah Arendt, without a recognition and practical acceptance of the plurality of human beings, it is scarcely possible to talk of a human condition. Certainly, it is impossible to talk in any significant sense about a human condition as something to be made. Arendt believes that: 'In man, otherness, which he shares with everything that is, and distinctness, which he shares with everything alive, become uniqueness, and human plurality is the paradoxical plurality of unique beings' (Arendt 1958: 156). Consequently, any failure to recognize plurality stands as something by way of a failure to acknowledge what it means to be human in the world with others.

The plurality of unique human beings is not just an ontological condition. It is also cultural. The cultural dimension is the practical response (the making of humanity) to the ontological condition (the finding of human beings). For Arendt, it is because of plurality that there is human action and, importantly, human speech: 'Through them, men distinguish themselves instead of being merely distinct; they are the modes in which human beings appear to each other, not indeed as physical objects, but *qua* men' (Arendt 1958: 156). This emphasis on action and speech means that: 'A life without speech and without action . . . is literally dead to the world; it has ceased to be a human life because it is no longer lived among men' (Arendt 1958: 157). But the social and cultural implication of enchantment and un-quiet is exactly one of human life becoming dead to the world. Enchantment means that human action becomes improbable in so far as it becomes decreasingly possible to identify and experience a specifically and peculiarly human context in which that action might be practised. Meanwhile, the environmental condition of un-quiet means that speech ceases to be a self-evidently immediate, direct and undistorted mode of communication between unique individuals. Un-quiet means that speech might not be audible. Yet the flight to the quiet of intimacy and contentment implies that the generality of other unique individuals ceases to be of necessary or inevitable moral concern.

The point I want to make is that if the human condition is one of human relationships, human fabrication and human negotiations with the being in the world of others, then the tendencies towards reification, enchantment, noise and the privacy of intimacy, can all be taken to stand as intimations of a condition which can only be called inhuman. It is inhuman because human being is rendered objectless (it is both social and natural at one and the same time without being entirely either). Human being is ordinary because uniqueness is impossible to construct. Human being is dead because it is no longer an existence with other humans who are anything more than things (things to the gaze and imagination; ironically those others are objectless in ontological terms. In all they are quite insubstantial).

All of this means that in existential terms life becomes very easy because there are few if any issues about which the individual feels that she or he might be able to make any kind of difference whatsoever. Action becomes little more than an occasional interruption of quiet contentment. After all, if the inhuman condition is one in which human being is dead to the world, there are no other unique beings with whom action is possible and no social and cultural problems which are experienced as liable to a social and cultural intervention. The individual is only able to experience uniqueness in a private sphere which is constructed around the enchantment of intimacy. Yet that turn to the private means that despite everything else existence can still be made sensible. Comfort need not be disrupted, and being in the here and now can be accepted as not all bad. And so, in place of the human condition with its cultural productions of action and speech, there emerges the inhuman condition with its cultural form of kitsch. Kitsch is the label I wish to apply to all cultural production, and thereby all existential experiences and emotions, which uphold the necessity of this way of life; which accept the inevitability of the existing reifications. Consequently, kitsch is the culture of and in second nature. If human being entails the experience of homesickness, the inhuman condition is the eternal promise, prospect and allure of home.

My use of the category of kitsch is indebted to the discussion of the concept which Milan Kundera provided in *The Unbearable Lightness of Being* and developed a little in *The Art of The Novel* (Kundera 1985, 1988. For a helpful collection of other accounts and analyses of kitsch see Dorfles 1969). Kundera deploys the category so that it becomes the most serious fault line between two different attitudes towards the world. According to Kundera, it is important and possible to identify a 'line separating those who doubt being as it is granted to man (no matter how or by whom) from those who accept it without reservation' (Kundera 1985: 247). On the one side of that line are to be found all of the social and cultural groups and all of the individuals who experience the world and existence in it through an acceptance and the choice of the critical distance allowed by alienation. These are the individuals and the groups who tend to experience themselves as living a life which is dominated by a sense of contingency in a world of contingency. They exist in experiential and perhaps even environmental situations of un-quiet. They are the homesick. On the other side of the line are all of those groups and individuals which and who tend to resort to, or are given no choice other than to accept, the quiet of contentment. They tend to experience the world as necessary, as the way it simply has to be. These are the groups and individuals that look to their being and 'who accept it without reservation'. It is this acceptance of being without reservation which is the basis of the kitsch which Kundera defines as 'a categorical agreement with being' (Kundera 1985: 248).

Kitsch offers a reason never to entertain doubt. It is precisely for this reason that Kundera calls it a categorical agreement with being. Kundera tries to spell out the meaning of this phrase when he writes that: 'the aesthetic ideal of the categorical agreement with being is a world in which shit is denied and everyone acts as though it did not exist. This aesthetic ideal is called kitsch'. More concisely yet: 'kitsch excludes everything from its perview which is essentially unacceptable in human existence' (Kundera 1985: 248). (In these terms kitsch is also the sensibility that it is unseemly to use a word like shit in a book of social and cultural theory.) Kundera uses the word shit in both its literal and its metaphorical senses. Kitsch involves the applauding of life as it is lived here and now as the only possible life which might be lived at any time in any place (and thus, metaphorically, it is an avoidance of the shit which life might often be). It is also an

135

avoidance of a confrontation with those aspects of existence which are socially and culturally defined as unedifying.

The categorical agreement with being has a number of aspects. Firstly, it involves an almost Panglossian acceptance of the myth that all is for the best in this, the best of all possible worlds (and this world must be the best possible world precisely because it has no place for shit; precisely because shit has been excluded from it). The world is flattened out so that everything which needs to be said and which can be said is taken to be quite self-evident. According to Kundera, in this situation: 'To please, one must confirm what everyone wants to hear, put oneself at the service of received ideas. Kitsch is the translation of the stupidity of received ideas into the language of beauty and feeling' (Kundera 1988: 163). Secondly, the categorical agreement with being entails a concentration on what is said to be the inner and transcendental truth of being. This inner truth is located in what are held to be the calls of the heart (and so here is a connection between kitsch and the enchantment of the emotions and of intimacy). Kitsch is that which 'moves us to tears of compassion for ourselves, for the banality of what we think and feel' (Kundera 1988: 163). According to Kundera in *The Unbearable Lightness of Being*: 'When the heart speaks, the mind finds it indecent to object. In the realm of kitsch, the dictatorship of the heart reigns supreme' (Kundera 1985: 250).

Kundera illustrates this reference to the dictatorship of the heart. At one point in Kundera's novel two of the characters are watching some children ice-skating and playing on the grass at a sports stadium. One of the two is moved virtually to tears by the sight he sees: 'describing a circle with his arm, a circle that was meant to take in stadium, grass, and children, he added, "Now, that's what I call happiness"' (Kundera 1985: 250). That is exactly what Kundera calls kitsch. The point is that this kind of response to the sight of children playing does not allow space and time for any critical encounter with the moment. Even less does it allow for any possibility that the sight might have a plurality of meanings or different meanings for the different participants. Instead the plurality of human being (of the human being of the children) is denied with an all-inclusive sweep of the arm. Moreover, this straightforward one-on-one identification of the viewer with viewed overcomes any possibility of a sense of alienation. The sweep of the arm is a movement of quiet, of acceptance and of agreement that this is the way the world should be. The kitsch sensibility only allows for an immediate response which derives its legitimacy and authority from its connection to what is taken to be the pre-reflexive truth which everyone feels in their heart of hearts. As such, kitsch is an agreement with life as it is lived and experienced, with existence as it is presently organized. It is an agreement which condemns any kind of critical action as distasteful, inappropriate or plain mischievous.

But the idea of the dictatorship of the heart has another implication. Since the heart is understood as expressing deep truths which are known by everyone, then the kitsch sensibility is one which is shared. It is, once again, a denial of human plurality and thereby a denial of the need for any human action whatsoever (and so, by extension, human being becomes something which itself is found not made). The kitsch sensibility is the basis of an experience of existence in common. It makes us all the same. Consequently, kitsch is parasitic on familiar situations, images and roles since these are taken to be the secret of what it is that all humans have in common irrespective of evident differences (and so love is one of the prime sites of kitsch; love is kitsch). According to Kundera: 'Kitsch may not, therefore, depend on an unusual situation; it must derive from the basic images people have engraved in their memories.' This treasury for kitsch combines stereotyped roles with banal images: 'the ungrateful daughter, the neglected father, children running on the grass, the motherland betrayed, first love' (Kundera 1985: 251).

It is important to be aware of the shape and implications of kitsch because it is the defining trait of cultural production and experiences of existence in situations of quiet and in worlds which have been subjected to the tendencies towards reification. Kitsch is so attractive and so useful because it invests life with a large measure of credibility. It allows us to be credulous in relation to the worlds we experience. It makes life easy because it bolsters the other dimensions of the quiet contentment which surrounds the individual who has retreated, and who has been able to retreat thanks to the control of material resources, into his or her own private little world. But it is exactly this charm of kitsch which makes it so much of an obstacle to any attempts to make the human condition human.

Kitsch is the aesthetic and ethical product of second nature; and it is also a primary means by which that second nature can be experienced and accepted as ever more seductive. Kitsch means that the individual never has to think about alternatives. Indeed, in the world of kitsch there is no alternative worth thinking about because everything important is vouchsafed by the heart. As such, kitsch stands as an enchantment of social and cultural relationships and thus it is an aspect of the inhuman. The question which consequently arises is whether there is any way out of the embrace of kitsch. The question is whether there is any conceivable way in which the human condition might be returned to human being and the acceptance through action of human plurality.

According to Matei Calinescu there is a way out. Calinescu reaches this conclusion at the end of an exploration of kitsch as an aesthetic form which makes it easier for individuals to exist in this world. He puts into a sentence a theme which runs all the way through Kundera's discussion of kitsch. Calinescu stresses the ability of kitsch to stimulate what feels like authenticity on the part of the individual who responds to certain familiar sights or things in an immediate and emotional way. For Calinescu the erstwhile authenticity implied in kitsch goes hand in hand with its increasing predominance as an aesthetic form: 'After all, in today's world no one is safe from kitsch, which appears as a necessary step on the path toward an ever elusive goal of fully authentic aesthetic experience' (Calinescu 1987: 262). It would seem that for Calinescu, who builds on foundations laid by Adorno, a considerable part of this ability of kitsch is attributable to the fact that it is not as boring as everyday life: 'the desire to escape from adverse or simply dull reality is perhaps the main reason for the wide appeal of kitsch' (Calinescu 1987: 237). Kitsch is attractive because it fills all the free time in which un-quiet thoughts might develop. Kitsch is a kind of aesthetic and environmental noise which produces emotional and psychological quiet. After all: 'spare time – whose quantity is socially increasing – is felt as a strange burden, the burden of emptiness'. And so: 'Kitsch appears as an easy way of "killing time," as a pleasurable escape from the banality of both work and leisure. The fun of kitsch is just the other side of terrible and incomprehensible boredom' (Calinescu 1987: 248). (Of course, it is not just work and leisure which might be boring; enforced non-work is liable to be extremely boring as well.)

Yet Calinescu sees the seeds of hope in this situation. For

Calinescu, kitsch 'is a world of aesthetic make-believe and self-deception' (Calinescu 1987: 262). This means that kitsch is to a significant extent parasitic upon artistic forms; kitsch tells us that we do not need to visit a gallery to see a painting by a 'great artist' since we can buy a reproduction to hang in our own homes. The reproduction of the painting will be something I can idly look at when I have nothing better to do. But, according to Calinescu, this means that kitsch can lead us to an appreciation of the value of the original: 'Offering "duplicates" of almost every known art form, kitsch suggests . . . the way toward the originals.' For example: 'After seeing many reproduced or fake Rembrandts, a viewer may ultimately be receptive to the experience of coming upon the real painting of a Dutch master.' The viewer, 'may finally become aware that art, even when exploited, misunderstood, and misused, does not lose its value and aesthetic truth' (Calinescu 1987: 262).

It is possible to see how Calinescu reaches this conclusion that in the end kitsch tends to subvert itself because it unintentionally demonstrates the value of original works of art. But Calinescu's argument is based on two assumptions which cannot be readily accepted if it is appropriate to define kitsch as the categorical agreement with being. Firstly, Calinescu assumes that the viewers of kitsch aesthetic forms, the inhabitants of kitsch culture, will for some reason or another find themselves in a place like an art gallery able to gaze upon and contemplate the significance of a Dutch painting. But there is no reason to assume that the individuals will go into a gallery and, even if they do, there is no reason at all to assume that they are there to look at the paintings. They could have entered the building for a cup of coffee or simply to visit the gift shop in order to demonstrate that they could have looked at the pictures if they had wanted to but they had something better to do instead. Secondly, Calinescu tends to assume that the qualities of the original work of art will be so obvious to any and every viewer that they will be able to identify it as the original. But if kitsch has taken the kind of deep aesthetic hold that Calinescu argues that it has, then it is not self-evident that the original will be recognized for what it is. Moreover, there is no reason to assume that the original will be accepted as the site of value. Inevitably the original will be compared to the reproduction which hangs on the wall at home and the original will quite probably be found to be somewhat lacking.

Treated as an aesthetic problem kitsch is an entirely self-sufficient world from which there would seem to be few chances of escape. To the extent that kitsch asserts a categorical agreement with being then, there seem to be few if any reasons to believe that individuals will want or be able to upset the safe certainties which they are able to experience. Kitsch makes the world make sense and, moreover, it allows the individual to believe that she or he is doing everything that she or he can rightly do. In other words, kitsch allows the individual to do nothing because there is no reason to do anything; within the kitsch situation there is no plurality of human beings that might constitute the context and cause of any action. The logic of Calinescu's position is that original works of art can disrupt all of this stupidity of received wisdom (to use a phrase of Kundera's), but in the last instance perhaps Calinescu's faith is based on little more than wishful thinking.

Kitsch combines with enchantment to produce and reproduce a social and cultural milieu which is experienced as like a seamless web which has no point of entry for human intervention. That is the essence of the experience of second nature; the accommodation to what is confronted as being there prior to and independently of any given individual. Such a conclusion implies a complete despair; a despair that the world has escaped human making such that the human condition is no longer able to maintain any specifically and differently human aspect. But the domination of kitsch, enchantment and, in all, the sway of second nature can be challenged. One of the chances of a challenge is generated by the maintenance amongst certain individuals and social and cultural groups of the state of mind of alienation. In this way some individuals and groups might be able to bear witness and say 'No' to the tendencies and processes of the dehumanization of what ought to be the human world. (Of course whether anyone will listen to the witnesses is another matter entirely; the kitsch situation is probably such that no one will, or will want to. Perhaps then the witnesses will either become so alienated that they will become entirely detached from the human condition become second nature or they will be subsumed within it. The former possibility is too heroic, the latter possibility is more probable because it is more easy.) Yet, much more generally than this, perhaps the human condition can be made human through an emphasis upon the body.

The body can never become entirely self-evident. It can never really be accorded an absolute and a final categorical agreement. The body always escapes social and cultural abilities to define it once and for all. There are two main aspects to this ability of the body. Firstly, the body is ambivalent because it straddles the milieux of both first and second nature. My body is a natural material object and yet I use and deploy it in socially and culturally learned subjective ways. But what I can learn is influenced by my natural qualities and my natural qualities only have significance in relation to social and cultural meanings. Secondly, the body possesses the ability to undermine social and cultural enterprises. The body can do unexpected things at unexpected times so that social and cultural enterprises might come to lose some of their taken-for-grantedness and authority. This possibility is of course a dominant theme in Dostoevsky's *Notes from Underground*, but it was very neatly expressed by Mayakovsky in his poem 'A Cloud in Trousers': 'I know – / a nail in my boot that's hurting / is nightmarish more than the fantasy of Goethe' (Mayakovsky 1965: 108). As such, it might well be through a consideration of the place of the body in social and cultural relationships and certainties that the inhuman condition of enchantment and kitsch might be challenged just a little bit.

Perhaps the finest testimony of the ambivalences and uncertainties of the body is to be found in the work of the painter Francis Bacon. As Bacon put the matter: 'we are meat, we are potential carcasses. If I go into a butcher's shop I always think it's surprising that I wasn't there instead of the animal' (Bacon quoted in Sylvester 1980: 46). For Bacon humanity is placed somewhere between a meathook and a shop; humanity is placed in the social and the cultural and the natural environments at one and the same time. Humanity is the meat and the butcher. In these terms it is possible to identify the paintings of Francis Bacon as an interpretation of existence which offers an alternative experience to that framed by the dull inhuman wisdom of the received ideas of the categorical agreement with being. Bacon forces a consideration of the question of the precise status and meaning of the being which seeks (or which has sought for it) categorical agreement in the first place.

According to his own statements at least, Bacon was concerned to paint in a way which communicates with sensations of existence and not with socially and culturally constructed stories. One

141

way he tried to do this was by eschewing all narrative in his paintings. Bacon said that he wanted 'very, very much to do the thing that Valéry said – to give the sensation without the boredom of its conveyance' (Bacon quoted in Sylvester 1980: 65). This concern to avoid narrative (and to 'therefore return the onlooker to life more violently'; Bacon quoted in Sylvester 1980: 17) can be taken as one explanation why so many of the figures in Bacon's paintings are isolated and quite alone: 'The moment there are several figures . . . the story begins to be elaborated. And the moment the story is elaborated, the boredom sets in' (Bacon quoted in Sylvester 1980: 22). With this claim Bacon is not primarily making some existentialist point about humanity being alone in the universe and neither is he painting about the absurdity of life. After all, such storytelling concerns would involve the implication of a narrative of truth behind the image. What he is trying to do is make the audience feel the painting at a sensual not intellectual level (this aspect of Bacon's work is emphasized in Boyne 1988). A rather unresolved irony with Bacon is that despite his refusal to paint stories the carefully chosen titles to his paintings (titles which often direct the audience to another text) do indeed invoke at least a minimal narrative element.

The effect of the reliance on the sensation of the painting on the part of the audience and the effect of the refusal to paint stories is that the meaning of the work is made less than entirely obvious. The meaning has to be made. Certainly, and obviously, Bacon paints material bodily forms which are highly distorted (it is possible to understand his paintings at that simple descriptive level) but the point he is trying to make with the distortion has to be constructed by the audience in an act of critical enquiry and reflection. He alienates the audience from what it sees; he makes the audience human. Bacon is not saying that human being, and the meaning of human being, is something which is waiting somewhere to be found; Bacon wants us to make human being for ourselves by paying attention to what it feels like to be human. I want to propose that with this concern Francis Bacon implies an alternative to any inevitability and longevity of the inhuman condition. Bacon opens up one avenue of the rehumanization of the world precisely because he makes us quite uncertain about what humanity is (and it is perhaps precisely confusion which defines our humanity). Bacon makes sure that our being can never be accorded a categorical agreement.

Although Bacon is undoubtedly concerned with the problem of what it means to be human, with what human being might mean, his art more specifically explores the problem of what it is and feels like to be human in the world that humans have made. This concern is reflected in Bacon's tendency to paint figures in claustrophobic pre-existing rooms (which are so well made that they are just found) and not the open air. As Lorenza Trucchi has written: 'Bacon's man prefers an artificial environment, as nondescript as possible, to the great womb of mother Earth' (Trucchi 1976: 4). Trucchi's observation is well made but the reckoning is slightly awry. It is not so much that Bacon's figures prefer the artificial-made-natural environment of social and cultural construction, it is rather that this is the only world on offer to them. They are fated to live in rooms which are often empty of others. Choice does not enter into the equation. Bacon shows that the rooms we all occupy for most of our lives might contain something other than the tamed and ritualized bodies with the distinguishable and objective attributes of kitsch forms and naturalized social and cultural relationships. Bacon's rooms contain bodies which always escape any pretence that they might be controlled by experts and expertise. The rooms might well contain suppurating meat. Bacon paints a situation in which, 'man now realizes that he is an accident, that he is a completely futile being, that he has to play the game without reason' (Bacon quoted in Sylvester 1980: 28). Bacon's situation is that of homesickness.

John Russell suggests that the rooms Bacon paints are themselves intimations of a purely contingent presence of the individual body in any given time and place (although the pre-existence of the room is indeed taken for granted): 'The Room is borrowed space . . . space on loan, space rented for a day or two . . . like the standard hotel-bedrooms or rented rooms in which so much of the inner life of our century has been played out' (Russell 1979: 75). Russell's comments about Bacon's rooms are reminiscent of T.S. Eliot's talk in 'The Love Song of J. Alfred Prufrock', 'Of restless nights in one-night cheap hotels' (Eliot 1954). (Bacon of course derived themes for some of his paintings from the work of Eliot; see Russell 1979: 145–148, 152. But perhaps the use of lonely rooms in cheap hotels or boarding houses is also somewhat reminiscent of themes from Graham Greene.)

Bacon locates the body, and indeed the human being, in what Gilles Deleuze calls '*a zone of indiscernibility* between man and the animal' (Deleuze 1983: 11). Bacon emphasizes the status of the body as a material presence which is experienced and apprehended as occupying two different environments at one and the same time. Consequently he constructs the body as human and yet also animal. The body is a problem to be confronted rather than a dull fact which can be accepted more or less at ease. Bacon is not saying anything as simple as that there is or might be a direct correspondence between the human and the animal. His painting is much more interesting than that. Perhaps Deleuze lapses into hyperbole but nevertheless he makes a good point when he says that with Bacon: 'Man becomes an animal, but only on condition that the animal at one and the same time become spirit, the spirit of man' (Deleuze 1983: 11). There can be no categorical agreement with being for the fundamental reason that it is impossible to know for sure what being might mean or even indeed what it might look like. Neither is Bacon making the crass point that the human body is an animal body. Instead he is forcing the spectator to consider for him or her self precisely what the status of the body might be.

This problematization of what it means to be a material being, this exacerbation of the problem of what the word 'human' might actually mean in material and even moral terms, is pushed even further by Bacon's way of painting the face. Bacon makes the face into something difficult. He makes it into something which cannot meet with any kind of agreement since its nature too is hard to understand. Bacon paints heads not faces. He paints 'the skull beneath the skin' (Eliot again; see 'Whispers of Immortality' in Eliot 1954). The distinction between the head and the face has been made by Gilles Deleuze (who would seem to have read the relevant pieces of Eliot as well). He writes that: 'The face is a structured spatial organization that covers the head, whereas the head is one of the body's dependencies, even though it is where the body comes to its highest point' (Deleuze 1983: 11). As such, Bacon's reduction of the face to the head implies also a reduction of human being to the natural body which kitsch forms ostensibly remove from any social and cultural consideration. Bacon 'pursues a very special project: to unmake the face, to discover or conjure up the head beneath the face' (Deleuze 1983: 11).

Yet even more that this, Bacon reduces the head to the gaping hole of the mouth. That mouth is not still nor silent. But neither does that mean that the mouth is thereby the organ of speech and of the communication of human uniqueness. Bacon turns the mouth into an orifice of an anguished scream or a 'lipless grin' (Eliot, 'Whispers of Immortality'). Gilles Deleuze makes a similar point when he writes that in Bacon's paintings the mouth, 'is no longer a particular organ, but rather the hole through which the entirety of the body escapes and through which flesh descends' (Deleuze 1983: 14).

Dawn Ades has proposed that Bacon derived his use of the image of the screaming mouth from the work of Georges Bataille. Bataille argues that expressions of the most powerful human emotions are represented in the contortions of the mouth. In these terms, the mouth is the place through and with which we express our human being and humanity. But Bataille also noted quite how similar the human mouth is to the mouth of animals. Ades quotes Bataille who wrote: 'On great occasions human life is concentrated bestially in the mouth, anger makes one clench one's teeth, terror and atrocious suffering make the mouth the organ of tearing cries.' Bataille went on to argue that in experiencing these 'great occasions', the individual lifts up the head, 'so that the mouth comes to be placed, so far as is possible, in the extension of the vertebral column, that is to say in the position it normally occupies in the animal constitution' (Bataille quoted in Ades 1985: 13). Through the mouth, and especially the screaming mouth, the most extreme human emotions are expressed yet in that expression we come closest to being like animals. This is indeed Deleuze's zone of indiscernibility: 'for it is not that man in his scream sinks to the level of animal, but that this animal element is necessary and a part of him' (Ades 1985: 15).

Bacon does much the same for the body as he does for the face. He explores the possibility that the body might also occupy the zone of indiscernibility between the milieux of first and second nature. Bacon does this by dismantling the body and putting it back together again in ways which jar and upset preconceived notions about what the body ought to be like and how it should be constituted. With Bacon: 'flesh descends from the bones and the bones elevate themselves above flesh'. What remains is meat: 'Meat is that state of the body in which the flesh and the bones come to a local confrontation instead of composing themselves into a structure' (Deleuze 1983: 12). This move of redescribing the human body in terms of what thus becomes its fundamental status as and of meat means that Bacon is once again able to create the space from which it might be possible to do something other than proclaim a categorical agreement with being.

Bacon's paintings do not allow for quiet and neither are they a salve to contentment. What Bacon manages to do is make his audience experience the paintings in a way which is in some sense beyond and outside of the boundaries of socially and culturally authorized narratives. Bacon forces us back onto our own resources to make any kind of sense of what he makes us see and, in so doing, he makes us make up meanings for ourselves. He indicates a means by which the world might be transformed from reification into fabrication, from enchantment to the basis of a specifically and exclusively human condition. According to his own statements, Bacon does all of this because of his refusal to paint narratives. But with his deconstruction and odd reconstruction of the material human body Bacon was doing something of greater analytic significance. Bacon's paintings serve to remove the Archimedean gaze from human being (since the gaze might now be flawed. It might only see half the picture and, in any case, it is not obvious what is being seen; the possibility of decisive Archimedean understanding thus becomes confounded). The paintings also imply the ejection of the audience from the quiet of contentment and enchantment if only because they suggest that nothing is self-evident, that nothing is enchanted because this is actually the world made by humanity not by Gods. As such, the audience might be alienated from the environments and experiences of quiet; audiences and individual spectators alike might be rather more forced into the adoption of a critical and questioning perspective on all that they are, all that they experience and know.

The possibility of the dissolution of the Archimedean point means the dissolution of the imaginative terrain from which it is possible to establish and practise the conceit that there can be a single and an all-encompassing knowledge of the meanings of human being. In other words, human being in the world ceases to be susceptible to any all-inclusive simplification such as that implied by abstractions like statistics and the ordering practices carried out on their backs. Humanity is released from the puppet show (the puppet show which is so often supported by certain kinds of sociology. Once again then it becomes clear that any human writing about social and cultural life will probably have little or no similarity with what passes as orthodox sociology).

Equally, the dissolution of the Archimedean point reinserts humanity and human being into action. Since there is no longer a single and universal truth of human being in the world, so the meaning of that being becomes something to be made through negotiation between distinct individuals. Speech becomes the means of re-establishing the human condition on the basis of an acceptance and embracing of action. And therefore, humans might be able to confront each other as unique beings, with their own things to say, their own meanings to communicate, their own individuality to practise, the individuality of others to respect. We can show who we are rather than what we have been made to be (for speech as a mode of the practical revelation of self, see Arendt 1958: 159).

All of this represents a re-emergence of the possibility of natality out of the dead world of reification. The world becomes something which humans can fabricate for themselves, in the context of human possibilities. As Hannah Arendt says: 'The fact that man is capable of action means that the unexpected can be expected from him, that he is able to perform what is infinitely improbable.' Arendt continues: 'And this again is possible only because each man is unique, so that with each birth something uniquely new comes into the world' (Arendt 1958: 158). Or, to quote Arendt at length, at her most human, at her most important:

> The miracle that saves the world, the realm of human affairs, from its normal, 'natural' ruin is ultimately the fact of natality, in which the faculty of action is ontologically rooted. It is, in other words, the birth of new men and the new beginning, the action they are capable of by virtue of being born. Only the full experience of this capacity can bestow upon human affairs faith and hope . . .
> (Arendt 1958: 222)

But can a few paintings really be expected to inspire so much?

BIBLIOGRAPHY

Ades, Dawn (1985) 'Web of Images', in *Francis Bacon*, London: The Tate Gallery.

Adorno, Theodor (1967) *Prisms*, trans. Samuel and Shierry Weber, London: Neville Spearman.

Aquinas, St Thomas (1989) *Summa Theologiae. A Concise Translation*, (ed.) Timothy McDermott, London: Eyre & Spottiswoode.

Aragon, Louis (1971) *Paris Peasant*, trans. Simon Watson Taylor, London: Jonathan Cape.

Arendt, Hannah (1958) *The Human Condition. A Study of the Central Dilemmas Facing Modern Man*, New York: Doubleday Anchor.

Barthes, Roland (1983) *A Barthes Reader*, (ed.) Susan Sontag, London: Fontana.

Bataille, Georges (1986) Special edition of the journal *October*, no. 36.

Bauman, Zygmunt (1988) *Freedom*, Milton Keynes: Open University Press.

—— (1991) *Modernity and Ambivalence*, Cambridge: Polity.

—— (1993) 'Philosophy for Everyday – Though not for Everyone', *Economy and Society*, 22 (1): 114–122.

Benjamin, Walter (1973) *Illuminations*, trans. Harry Zohn, London: Fontana.

—— (1983) *Charles Baudelaire. A Lyric Poet in the Era of High Capitalism*, trans. Harry Zohn, London: Verso.

—— (1989) 'Surrealism: The Last Snapshot of the European Intelligentsia', in Stephen E. Bronner and Douglas McKay Kellner (eds), *Critical Theory and Society. A Reader*, New York: Routledge.

Berger, Peter, Berger, Brigitte and Kellner, Hansfried (1974) *The Homeless Mind*, Harmondsworth: Penguin.

Boyne, Roy (1988) 'The Art of the Body in the Discourse of Postmodernity', *Theory, Culture and Society*, 5: 527–542.

Brecht, Bertolt (1973) 'Binocular Vision in the Theatre: The Alienation Effect', in Elizabeth and Tom Burns (eds), *Sociology of Literature and Drama*, Harmondsworth: Penguin.

Buck-Morss, Susan (1977) *The Origin of Negative Dialectics. Theodor W. Adorno, Walter Benjamin, and the Frankfurt Institute*, New York: The Free Press.

—— (1989) *The Dialectics of Seeing. Walter Benjamin and the Arcades Project*, Cambridge, Mass.: The MIT Press.

Calinescu, Matei (1987) *Five Faces of Modernity. Modernism, Avant-Garde, Decadence, Kitsch, Postmodernism*, Durham: Duke University Press.

Deleuze, Gilles (1983) 'Francis Bacon: The Logic of Sensation', *Flash Art*, 112: 8–16.

Dorfles, Gillo (1969) *Kitsch: The World of Bad Taste*, New York: Universe Books.

Dostoevsky, Fyodor (1974) *Notes from Underground*, trans. Mirra Ginsburg, New York: Bantam Books.

Elias, Norbert (1978) *The History of Manners. The Civilizing Process Volume 1*, trans. Edmund Jephcott, Oxford: Basil Blackwell.

Eliot, T.S. (1954) *Selected Poems*, London: Faber & Faber.

—— (1982) 'Little Gidding' in *The Faber Book of Modern Verse*, Fourth Edition, London: Faber & Faber.

Fehér, Ferenc (1987) 'Freedom and the "Social Question" (Hannah Arendt's theory of the French Revolution)', *Philosophy and Social Criticism*, 12 (1): 1–30.

Foucault, Michel (1970) *The Order of Things. An Archaeology of the Human Sciences*, London: Tavistock.

—— (1979) *The History of Sexuality. Volume 1: An Introduction*, trans. Robert Hurley, London: Allen Lane.

Galbraith, John Kenneth (1992) *The Culture of Contentment*, London: Sinclair-Stevenson.

Game, Ann (1991) *Undoing the Social. Towards a Deconstructive Sociology*, Buckingham: Open University Press.

Giddens, Anthony (1993) *The Giddens Reader*, (ed.) Philip Cassell, London: Macmillan.

Hacking, Ian (1982) 'Biopower and the Avalanche of Printed Numbers', *Humanities in Society*, 5 (3 and 4): 279–295.

Harrington, Michael (1985) *The New American Poverty*, London: Firethorn.

Haug, Wolfgang Fritz (1986) *Critique of Commodity Aesthetics*, trans. Robert Bock, Cambridge: Polity.

Heidegger, Martin (1978) *Basic Writings*, (ed.) David Farrell Krell, London: Routledge & Kegan Paul.

—— (1993) '"Only a God Can Save Us": *Der Spiegel*'s Interview with Martin Heidegger (1966)', in Richard Wolin (ed.), *The Heidegger Controversy: A Critical Reader*, Cambridge, Mass.: The MIT Press.

Heller, Agnes (1990) *Can Modernity Survive?* Cambridge: Polity.

Heller, Agnes and Fehér, Ferenc (1988) *The Postmodern Political Condition*, Cambridge: Polity.

Huizinga, Johan (1955) *The Waning of the Middle Ages*, Harmondsworth: Penguin.

Jonas, Hans (1984) *The Imperative of Responsibility. In Search of an Ethics for the Technological Age*, Chicago: University of Chicago Press.

Kermode, Frank (1973) 'Literary Fiction and Reality', in Elizabeth and Tom Burns (eds), *Sociology of Literature and Drama*, Harmondsworth: Penguin.

BIBLIOGAPHY

Kundera, Milan (1985) *The Unbearable Lightness of Being*, trans. Michael Henry Heim, London: Faber & Faber.

—— (1988) *The Art of the Novel*, trans. Linda Asher, London: Faber & Faber.

Levinas, Emmanuel (1988) *The Provocation of Levinas. Rethinking the Other*, (ed.) Robert Bernasconi and David Wood, London: Routledge.

Lukács, Georg (1971) *History and Class Consciousness. Studies in Marxist Dialectics*, trans. Rodney Livingstone, London: Merlin Press.

—— (1978) *The Theory of the Novel. A Historico-Philosophical Essay on the Forms of Great Epic Literature*, trans. Anna Bostock, London: Merlin Press.

Marx, Karl (1938) *Capital. A Critical Analysis of Capitalist Production. Volume 1*, London: George Allen & Unwin.

—— (1977) *Economic and Philosophic Manuscripts of 1844*, Moscow: Progress Publishers.

Mayakovsky, Vladimir (1965) *Mayakovsky*, trans. and (ed.) Herbert Marshall, London: Dennis Dobson.

Morawski, Stefan (1994) 'The Hopeless Game of Flânerie', in Keith Tester (ed.) *The Flâneur*, London: Routledge.

Orwell, George (1984) *The Penguin Essays of George Orwell*, Harmondsworth: Penguin.

Pascal, Blaise (1931) *Pensées*, London: Everyman.

Perec, Georges (1990) *Things. A Story of the Sixties*, trans. David Bellos, London: Collins Harvill.

Russell, John (1979) *Francis Bacon*, London: Thames & Hudson.

Sartre, Jean-Paul (1958) *Being and Nothingness. An Essay on Phenomenological Ontology*, trans. Hazel E. Barnes, New York: Philosophical Library.

Schivelbusch, Wolfgang (1980) *The Railway Journey. Trains and Travel in the 19th Century*, trans. Anselm Hollo, Oxford: Basil Blackwell.

Shields, Rob (1992) 'Spaces for the Subject of Consumption', in Rob Shields (ed.), *Lifestyle Shopping. The Subject of Consumption*, London: Routledge.

Simmel, Georg (1950) *The Sociology of Georg Simmel*, trans. and (ed.) Kurt H. Wolff, New York: The Free Press.

—— (1969) 'Sociology of the Senses: Visual Interaction', in Robert E. Park and Ernest W. Burgess (eds), *Introduction to the Science of Sociology*, Third Edition, Chicago: University of Chicago Press.

Sylvester, David (1980) *Interviews with Francis Bacon, 1962–1979*, London: Thames & Hudson.

Tester, Keith (1992) *Civil Society*, London: Routledge.

Trucchi, Lorenza (1976) *Francis Bacon*, trans. John Shepley, London: Thames & Hudson.

Turner, Bryan (1984) *The Body and Society*, Oxford: Basil Blackwell.

Turner, Stephen P. and Kasler, Dirk (1992) *Sociology Responds to Fascism*, London: Routledge.

Walzer, Michael (1989) *The Company of Critics. Social Criticism and Political Commitment in the Twentieth Century*, London: Peter Halban.

Weber, Max (1930) *The Protestant Ethic and the Spirit of Capitalism*, trans. Talcott Parsons, London: George Allen & Unwin.

—— (1948) *From Max Weber. Essays in Sociology*, (ed.) Hans Gerth and C. Wright Mills, London: Routledge & Kegan Paul.

Wolff, Kurt H. (1988) 'The Idea of Surrender-and-Catch Applied to the Phenomenon of Karl Mannheim', *Theory, Culture and Society*, 5 (4): 715–734.

—— (1989) 'From Nothing to Sociology', *Philosophy of the Social Sciences*, 19 (3): 321–339.

Zweig, Stefan (1943) *The World of Yesterday*, London: Cassell.

INDEX